Reading Between the
Letters of the Gospels

Reading Between the Letters of the Gospels

MARK C. KILEY

WIPF & STOCK · Eugene, Oregon

READING BETWEEN THE LETTERS OF THE GOSPELS

Copyright © 2024 Mark C. Kiley. All rights reserved. Except for brief quotations in critical publications or reviews, no part of this book may be reproduced in any manner without prior written permission from the publisher. Write: Permissions, Wipf and Stock Publishers, 199 W. 8th Ave., Suite 3, Eugene, OR 97401.

Wipf & Stock
An Imprint of Wipf and Stock Publishers
199 W. 8th Ave., Suite 3
Eugene, OR 97401

www.wipfandstock.com

PAPERBACK ISBN: 979-8-3852-0124-2
HARDCOVER ISBN: 979-8-3852-0125-9
EBOOK ISBN: 979-8-3852-0126-6

VERSION NUMBER 08/30/24

Contents

Introduction | vii

Pentateuchal Unity in Matthew 1 and 2 | 1
Yhwh in the Servant Poems of Isaiah and in Matthew 4—12 | 4
Without a Wedding Garment: A Note on Matthew 22:12 | 13
Skylla, Charybdis, and Planktae in Mark 5—7 | 16
K-L-B in Mark 7 | 19
"...And having spit..." (Mark 7:33 and 8:23) | 22
Where and what is Dalmanoutha? (Mark 8:10) | 24
Job 29 in Mark 9:1–29 | 28
Subtext and Intertext in Mark 16:1—8 | 30
Follow the feet (Luke 7:36–50) | 43
The Intercalated Splendor of Luke's
 Conversation with Aratos | 49
Letters, the Writing, and the Rock in John 7 | 85
The Beloved Disciple, Judas Iscariot | 88
The Johannine Paraclete as an Index of Sorts | 135
Intercalated ἱλαστήριον/ Mercy Seat in John 19:13, 14 | 146

Šemeš at the cross of Jesus (John 19:29) | 148

Afterword: Some Questions about Jacob
    Jordaens *The Four Evangelists* | 151

Bibliography | 153
Ancient Document Index | 159

Introduction

THE TITLES OF THE following essays, crafted over the course of the years since their predecessors of 2012, are self-explanatory to some degree. They deal with problematic aspects of Gospel narratives that have bothered me for some time and I discuss them for the most part in terms based on the most recent critically received manuscripts in both the canonical Jewish Scriptures and New Testament. However, at some point in many of them, I also pay attention to individual letters that occur in a sequence correctly ordered, forming words that provide subtext pertinent to the main text. This did not start out as a planned attack on form criticism but it has effectively turned out to put form critics' concerns in a more holistic context. That is, while attention to form across many different texts and periods of antiquity gives us some sense of the generic identity of a narrative pericope, it does not of itself attend to the specifics, the finely crafted detail, that make two texts the same but different. That is more the job of redaction criticism and I suggest that attending to intercalation, the sprinkling of letters in the correct order through a patch of discrete already integral words, offers a new task for redaction criticism, one having affinities with the work of those who study the poetics of antiquity. Whether the reader finds one or another reading convincing is of course his or her choice but I would hope that at least 60% of the readings of intercalated subtext will meet with the reader's approval. While remaining only commentary on the main text, this reading tactic

INTRODUCTION

presents an extra level of what the narratives present. Therefore, to the extent that this roll of the die puts down anchor on a beach at the border of previous and new readings, I retain the initial dedication of the 2012 collection: To Tomorrow's Researchers in New Testament and Christian Origins.

Finally, a brief practical tip and a longer indication of thanks. While I will be working with the Hebrew and Greek texts as such, the only skill required of the reader is the ability to identify similarly shaped letters. In those instances when the Greek of a verse is mentioned but not rendered in this study, I refer the reader to the growing abundance of online resources for gaining access to the original languages of the Scriptural texts.[1] Let visual intelligence have its sway.

It is also my duty and pleasure to thank those who have made these pages possible, beginning with the capable and generous staff at Wipf and Stock, especially Matthew Wimer, and Emily and George Callihan. Thanks are due to the staff of the Loretto Library on the Staten Island Campus of St. John's University, New York, persevering in a period when the library faces an uncertain future: Diana Cerullo, Lois Cherepon, Ann Jusino, Mary Ann Lach, Marian Mercante, and Carmela Parvis. Thanks also to Matthew Baker and staff at the helm of the beautifully restored reading room of the Union Theological Library on the Columbia University campus, and for the staff (and resplendent surroundings) of the successfully renovated Rose Reading Room at the New York Public Library, Forty-Second Street. A special thank you to my colleagues, and Chair Rev. Patrick Flanagan, in the Department of Theology and Religious Studies at St John's as well as to Dean Teresa Delgado who defended my recent application for a Professional Development leave with benefits. To members of the Catholic Biblical Association and Society of Biblical Literature, especially those in the Hebrew Bible and New Testament Seminars at Columbia University, who have been

---

1. Septuagint online https://diebibel.ibep-prod.com/en/bible/LXX/EXO.3 as well as the Society of Biblical Literature Greek New Testament in the drop-down menu of ALL in https://biblegateway.com.

Introduction

unstinting in sharing their constructive critiques with me. To the Eucharistic community at St. Francis Xavier parish with whom I pray for church and world. To each of my students at St. John's Staten Island, and to my brother Den and sister Teresa who have borne my regular progress reports with equanimity. And to those on the street who have accompanied the growth of the manuscript with mummery, from the young man mimicking pregnancy to the young woman sporting a suspiciously replete cranial gauze bandage to the gentleman doing a tight circumpolar orbit around a traffic sign on Sixth Avenue, *grazie*. The Theatah is dead; long live The Theatah.

Mark C. Kiley
Staten Island, NY
September 30, 2023

Pentateuchal Unity in Matthew 1 and 2

ALL OF THE CRITICAL commentaries report dutifully that the infancy narratives in Matthew are punctuated by quotes of or references to the Prophets. However, Matthew's Jesus summarizes the tradition as "the Law and the Prophets" (7:12). "The Law" refers to the Law of Moses as interpreted by Jesus. In this critical note, I suggest that undergirding the explicit prophetic structure of Matthew 1 and 2, there is an implicit substructure of the Law of Moses, the Pentateuch. How does that thesis work?

In the columns below, I trace explicit quotes in Matthew 1 and 2. Near them, in italicized CAPITAL Letters, I trace the implicit presence of successive books of the Pentateuch:

A] Matthew 1 and 2:
B] Matthew 1:18—25
Isaiah 7:14—"she will conceive and bear a son . . . Emmanuel" is quoted at Matthew 1:23.

GENESIS: [The Greek *phrase* Βίβλος γενέσεως/Book of Origin, cited in Matt 1:1 reflects the name of the first book of the Pentateuch, as does Matt 1:18 which uses the word γενεσις]. Genesis contains multiple accounts of childbearing and family trees. Matthew begins with a genealogy.

B] Matthew 2:1—12

Micah-Micah 5:1a about a leader (Hebrew מֹושֵׁל) mōšēl in Israel is quoted by Matthew 2:6. Immediately following in Micah 5:1b LXX the Greek version, not explicitly quoted by Matthew, says "... and his *exodoi/ exits, goings out* are from ancient times ..."

EXODUS (Exodos), King Herod's malicious order to hunt for the newborn king in Matt 2:1–12, intending to have him killed, is a clear and *explicit* parallel to the order of Pharaoh in Exodus 1 to kill the newborns of the Hebrews. Moses as an infant is spared that fate. The material that Matthew quotes from Micah and its context in Micah is an *implicit* echo of the Exodus theme and perhaps a reminder of the name of Moses.

The letters of the name of the book of Ἔξοδος are present here in Matt 2:11.

Begin at προσεκύνησαν and end at σμύρναν:

¹¹ προσεκύνησαν ... ἀνοίξαντες ... τοὺς ... δῶρα ... χρυσὸν ... σμύρναν.

B] Matthew 2:13—15

Hosea 11:1—"Out of Egypt I have called my son" is quoted at Matt 2:15. The language of Jesus leaving Egypt by a "call" reflects the opening of the third book of the Pentateuch, that is, *Leviticus*:

LEVITICUS 1:1 " The Lord called ... ..."

The letters of the name of the Book of Λευιτικον are present in Matt 2:13.

Begin at παράλαβε and end at ζητεῖν:

¹³ παράλαβε ... αὐτοῦ καὶ ... Αἴγυπτον καὶ ... ἐκεῖ ... σοι ... ζητεῖν

B] Matthew 2:16—18

Jeremiah—The lament over slain children in Matt 2:18 is drawn from Jeremiah 31:15. Herod's order given to soldiers to kill children of two years age or younger is recorded in Matt 2:16. Certain features of the slaughter of children up to 2 years old are

Pentateuchal Unity in Matthew 1 and 2

approximated in the opening of Numbers, standing fourth among the Books of Moses.

NUMBERS 1: features the design of the Hebrew army's fighting men from twenty years old and upward.

The letters of the name of the Book of Αριθμοι are present in Matthew 2:16–18.

Begin at πᾶσι (vs. 16) and end at καὶ (vs. 18):

^{16} πᾶσι ... ὁρίοις ... ἐπληρώθη ... Ἰερεμίου ... καὶ

B] Matthew 2:19—23

"What was spoken through the prophets" in Matt 2:23 is not a quote from *Deuteronomy*, the fifth Book of the Pentateuch. However, in Deuteronomy, the Word *prophet* occurs ten times. This occurs in Deuteronomy alone among the books of the Pentateuch. There are ten words in the Greek phrase at 2:23b "so that what was spoken through the prophets might be fulfilled "he will be called a Ναζωραῖος'": [ὅπως πληρωθῇ τὸ ῥηθὲν διὰ τῶν προφητῶν ὅτι Ναζωραῖος κληθήσεται].

The letters of the name of the Book of Δευτερονομιον are present in vss. 19 –23.

Begin at δὲ and end at ἀντὶ:

^{19} δὲ τοῦ ... φαίνεται ... ἐν ^{20} Ἐγερθεὶς ... τὸ παιδίον ... α ὑτοῦ ... μητέρα ... καὶ ^{22} ἀκούσας ... ἀντὶ

Note also that the first three vowel sounds of Ναζωραῖος in Matt 2:23 are the same vowels employed in the Hebrew circumlocution ᾽Ădōnay chosen in speech to preserve a sense of reverence for the Tetragrammaton itself. The Hebrew letters of the Tetragrammaton are a structuring principle in the Servant poems of Isaiah and in the summaries of Jesus' ministry in Matthew 4–12, for which see the accompanying essay in this collection.

Yhwh in the Servant Poems of Isaiah and in Matthew 4—12

THE FOLLOWING OBSERVATIONS DO not focus on the longstanding debate over the human identity of the Servant in Isaiah's Servant Poems. Rather, these observations here are properly theological, centered on the function of the Hebrew Name Yhwh in both the Servant Poems of Isaiah and Matthew 4-12. To the best of my knowledge, this question has not previously been discussed and proceeds here under the following headings:

> Quaternity and Yhwh in the Servant Poems
> Alphabetic rationale for the location of the Servant Poems in Isaiah
> Yhwh and four Matthean summaries of the ministry of Jesus
> Servants of Yhwh and "coming after" in Isaiah and Matthew

QUATERNITY AND YHWH IN THE FOUR SERVANT POEMS

The Servant Songs as identified by Bernhard Duhm (1922) are comprised of these four texts: 42:1-4; 49:1-6; 50:4-9 and

52:13—53:12.[1] Each bears within itself a fourfold repetition. There is some variation in the manner of expressing the quaternity (see Isa 50:4-9 below), but there is a discernible pattern of fours structuring each of the four poems.

42:1—4 my—my servant, my chosen one, my soul delights, my spirit.

49:1—6 Yhwh

> Yhwh called me from birth (vs. 1)
> My reward is with Yhwh (vs. 4)
> Now Yhwh has spoken (vs. 5)
> I am made glorious in the sight of Yhwh (vs. 5b)

50: 4-9 Adonay (Yhwh)

> 'Ădōnay Yhwh has given me (vs. 4)
> 'Ădōnay Elohim opens my ear (vs. 5)[2]
> 'Ădōnay Yhwh is my help (vs. 7)
> 'Ădōnay Yhwh is my help (vs. 9)

52:13—53:12 Yhwh

> To whom has the arm of Yhwh been revealed? (53:1)
> Yhwh has laid on him the guilt of us all (vs. 6)
> Yhwh was pleased to crush him in infirmity (vs. 10)

---

1. Duhm, *Das Buch Jesaja*, 19, 311. One of the subsequent explorations of the Poems in a monograph may be found in Kaufmann, *Babylonian Captivity*, 12–57. I follow here the readings of the most complete of the Isaiah scrolls found at Qumran, 1QIs-a. The manuscript itself is available online, and a translation into English with critical apparatus may be found in Abegg, Flint and Ulrich, eds. *Dead Sea Scrolls Bible*. The scroll as presented there displays some slight discrepancies from the Masoretic text.

2. 1QIs-a at Qumran reads "'Ădōnay 'Ĕlōhîm" in vs. 5. However, both vss. 4 and 5 concern the opening of the ear. I read this as an intentional gesture toward the Shema of Deuteronomy 6:4 "Hear O Israel, the Lord our God, the Lord is ONE." i.e. The Qumran scroll at Isa 50:5 alludes to the Name Yhwh for which 'Ădōnay is a circumlocution, in a manner appropriate to the focus on hearing that Name. Also note that this quatrain of first-person doublets is followed by another voice in the third person describing the servant of Yhwh (vs. 10). For these Names in the canonical picture at large, see Harvey, *Yhwh Elohim: A Survey of Occurrences*.

The pleasure of Yhwh shall be accomplished through him (vs. 10b)

These examples of quaternity subtly draw attention to the letters of Yhwh: The repetition of "my" involves the use of *yôd*, which is the first letter of Yhwh. The simple fourfold pattern of Yhwh occurs both in the second and in the fourth Song, precisely where the *hê* occurs in Yhwh. And the fourfold occurrence of 'Ădōnay, added to YHWH, points to the additive function of the conjunction *wāw*, and thence to the *wāw* in Yhwh.³

ALPHABETIC RATIONALE FOR THE LOCATION OF THE SERVANT SONGS IN ISAIAH

One of the theoretical hindrances to perceiving the unity of the Songs has been the fact that chapter 42 is so far removed from the latter three songs in chapters 49–53. However, the Hebrew alphabet offers a rationale for this arrangement. The first ten letters of the alphabet contain all of the letters in Yhwh. And the alphabetic distance between the initial yôd of Yhwh and the remaining letters hê-wāw-hê is approximated in the distance between Isaiah 42 and Isaiah 49–53:

Yôd—Ṭêt—Ḥêt—Zayin—**Wāw**—**Hê**—Dālet—Gîmel—Bêt—'Ālep

Put another way, the cluster of the last three Songs is placed at a distance that approximates the alphabetic distance between **Yôd** and **Hê—Wāw**.

Interestingly, too, after one shifts direction from the alphabetic sequence yôd to hê (in the move from 42–49) to the reverse alphabetic sequence in the move from heh to waw (in 49–50), it is then that we see 52:8 discussing the "return of the Lord."

---

3. It may also be the case that the *four* occurrences in Isaiah of the imperative form of q-š-b "take heed" (Is 10:30, 28:23, 34:1, 49:1) are riffing on the Shema. Such an allusion to the Tetragrammaton in 49:1 would signal that the Name is indeed of concern in the Servant poems.

Yod	Heh	Waw	Heh
Isaiah 42	← 49	→ 50	← 52—53

The spacing of the Songs limns the author's alphabetic progress through the letters of the Name Yhwh. If this is so, if the Prophet reflects Yhwh in the use of quaternity, informs the Songs by mimicking the second and fourth position of the Letter HEH in Yhwh, and spaces the Songs to reflect the distance of these letters from each other in the alphabet, one might expect explicit attention to the theme of "Name" as such. What do we see?

The "Name" שֵׁם –

Šem—with divine referent occurs just outside the first and third poems, in 42:8 and 50:10. It also occurs in 54:5, but that is not in as close proximity to the Fourth poem as is true of the first and third poems. The placement of the theme of the Name in varying degrees of proximity to the poems proper would be consonant with an exercise of the poetic craft in that the key unlocking the poems' unity is revealed, but not too blatantly.

Of course, these observations do not exhaust the range of other questions that may be asked of the poems.[4] One might wonder, for example, whether the names Isaiah and Hezekiah function as semaphores of the divine Name in the account of healing in Isaiah 37-39, and thus prepare for the Servant's profile that is thoroughly imbued with the saving presence of the Name. One might also ask about the portrayals of Elisha and Jeremiah in the construction of the profiles of the Servant.[5] Moreover, once the Isaianic poet has

---

4. One of the most comprehensive studies of the poems is available in North, *The Suffering Servant*. A sweeping survey of the Name itself, including its presence in the poems, is available in Parke-Taylor, *Yahweh: The Divine Name*. See also Rosel, "Names of God," 600-602.

5. Elisha in 2 Kings 1-13 offers several suggestive parallels with the Servant poems: His association with disciples of the prophets, the congruity between the scenes of supplying oil when it had run out and raising a mortally ill child and the poems' language "a bent reed he will not break nor will he quench a smoldering wick," the scene involving the sickness and arrow at the end of his life. Parallels with the portrait of Jeremiah have been ably examined by Dell, "The Suffering Servant," 119-34.

emphasized the Name's yôd in chapter 42 and wāw in chap. 50, he begins to populate Isaiah 50 with echoes of Lamentations.[6] Why? Perhaps because the Hebrew אוֹי, woe, is present in Lamentations, for example at 5:16, and it contains these two letters of the divine Name. That is, two of the letters of Yhwh, yôd and wāw, are given a role in shaping Second Isaiah's poems in part through a discourse with *Lamentations*. The Servant poems also generate continuing interest within the literature of Second Temple Judaism.[7] However, these subsidiary questions neither advance nor negate the full dimensions of the unifying presence of YHWH in the Servant poems as a group.[8]

YHWH AND FOUR MATTHEAN SUMMARIES OF THE MINISTRY OF JESUS

I suggest here that the four Servant Poems of Second Isaiah shape in part Matthew's summaries of Jesus' ministry in Matt 4–12. This thesis takes its cue from an article by Richard Beaton in which he says that Matthew has four summary passages of the ministry of Jesus.[9] Two quote servant songs. I would add that the other 2 summaries engage the other Servant Songs in Isaiah, reaching a crescendo in Matthew 12:21 *and the nations shall hope in his Name*.

Aspects of the four summary passages reflect the sequence of the letters in Yhwh:

---

6. For the echoes of Lamentations 3 in Isaiah 50, see Paul *Isaiah 40–66*, 350.

7. For example, Suggs, "Wisdom of Solomon 2:10—5:23," 26–33. Also see the survey "The Many Faces of the Servant of the Lord" chapter 8 in Blenkinsopp, *Opening the Sealed Book*, 251–93.

8. Wilkinson, *Tetragrammaton* is comprehensive in many ways but does not treat this interaction of Isaiah and Matthew.

9. Beaton, "Messiah and Justice," 5–23.

Yhwh in the Servant Poems of Isaiah and in Matthew 4—12

Yhwh	Matthew
YOD	4: ten
HEH	8: quotes poem of Isaiah 52, 53 that begins *hinnēh*
WAW	9: Kai/and 6x
HEH	12: quotes poem of Isaiah 42 that begins *hēn*

Yod is the 10th letter of the alphabet. Matt 4:23–25 places the Ten Cities at the center of its listed geographical designations i.e. Galilee–Syria–Galilee–*Ten Cities*–Jerusalem –Judea–Jordan. Moreover, the 3 areas beginning with I—Jerusalem, Judea, Jordan—mimic the sound of initial yôd in YHWH. And the Greek root for silence, sig- is present in the Galilee-Syria notations. Silence is an appropriate response to the presence of the Name.

Heh is the first letter of hinneh /behold in Isa 52:13—53:12, quoted in Matt 8:17. **Waw** is the sixth letter of the Hebrew alphabet and can mean "and". It is mirrored in the six instances of και in Matt 9:35–36.

Heh is the first letter of hinneh behold in Isa 42:1–4, quoted in Matt 12:18–21.

Just as the four Servant poems of Isaiah reflect engagement with the Name, so too Matthew's use of those four Servant Songs reflects engagement with the Name, the Tetragrammaton Yhwh. The Servant poems are structured with attention to groupings of four, orchestrated such that clusters two and four are similar to each other. In Matthew, summaries two and four are also similar to each other by dint of their quotations of Isaiah's Servant Songs. This arrangement mirrors the h of Yhwh. There is some congruity between summaries one and three in that they report some combination of Jesus' teaching-healing-synagogues.

Moreover, the Evangelist has embedded these explorations of the name Yhwh in material that resembles one or another of the Isaianic poems, though in these details discussed below Matthew follows a sequence different from the sequence of their occurrence in Isaiah:

Isaiah	Matthew
42 Behold my	12 behold (8x), my (11x)
49 To nations	4 Israel's neighbors
50 Learning Disciples למודים	9 learning disciples[10] μαθητης
52,5 For the many	8 Mark 1:29–34 many healed; brought to Matthew 8 out of sequence as compared with Mark

One may also find allusion to the Name Yhwh in the fact that the second and fourth beatitudes in Matthew 5 both highlight the same two letters in the Greek: pe

Penthous (mourn)

Peinōntes (hunger)

This limns the identical letter, in this case, hê, in the second and fourth letters of Yhwh.

Furthermore, the Name at the heart of Isaiah's Servant poems is comprised of the first ten letters of the twenty-four-letter Hebrew alphabet. The Matthean riff on Isaiah's Name-and-Servant occurs within the first twelve chapters of its twenty-eight chapters. i.e. the exercise in Matthew reaches to a little less than halfway through Matthew, as the Isaian exploration of the Name and Servant reaches to a little less than halfway through the Hebrew alphabet.

Reflecting the alphabetic distance between the Name's yôd and hê—wāw, the space between the first narrative riff on the Name and the remaining three riffs is marked in both Isaiah and Matthew. Compare the space between Isaiah 42 and Isaiah 49, 50, 53 and that between Matthew 4 and Matthew 8, 9, 12.

Congruent with the alignment of the Name and the name of Jesus is the fact that Matthew has eliminated those instances in his

---

10. Kiley, "Why 'Matthew,'" 47–51.

Markan base in which people address Jesus by name. The name Iēsous is a semaphore meaning "The Lord saves." The Gadarene demoniacs in Matt 8:28—34 (a single person in Mark 5) address Jesus as Son of God, not "Jesus." Matthew thereby seems to reflect the practice among some observant Jewish believers of refraining from pronouncing Yhwh, in favor of the circumlocution "Lord." And unlike Mark's Bartimaeus in Mark 10 who addresses Jesus as "Jesus", Matthew relates a story of blind men in Matt 9:27–31 who, together address Jesus as Son of David, but not as "Jesus."[11]

SERVANTS OF YHWH AND "COMING AFTER" IN ISAIAH AND MATTHEW

Michael Lyons has explored the ways in which the singular Servant has generated interest among the subsequent adherents of the Isaiah tradition, such that they consider themselves servants who share some of his profile.[12] He points to phrases in what he designates Trito-Isaiah "servants" (65:13, 14) "my chosen ones" (65:15) as indicating the self-identification of this group with the Servant. And he suggests that the same tradition is continued in aspects of Psalm 22: divine abandonment, remembrance of divine presence from the time of the womb, and the seed of Jacob who serve. I fully agree.

And I would add that Matthew stands in the tradition of acknowledging servants of the Servant. This he effects by populating his text with sixteen mentions of servants in the plural, more than in any of the other canonical Gospels. And they begin to appear

---

11. Two studies of the reception history of the Isaian Servant poems in Matthew seem especially noteworthy: Beaton, *Isaiah's Christ*. That study focuses on the poem in Isaiah 42 and as cited in Matthew 12. Shepherd, *Theological Interpretation* compares the theological presuppositions of three authors regarding the degree to which they privilege the text or dogmatic considerations. In addition, Holladay "Jesus' Ministry," 313-36 continues a long tradition that recognizes the increase in Matthew's use of "Lord" for Jesus in these chapters but is innocent of any reflection on its possible relation to Yhwh in the Servant poems.

12. Lyons, "Psalm 22 and the Servants," 640-66.

en masse after chapter 12: (Matt 13:27, 28; 14:2; 18:23; 21:34,35,36; 22:3,4,6,8,10,13; 25:14,19; 26:58). That is, having finished the bulk of his initial portrait of *The Servant*, the Evangelist begins to treat the theme of *servants*.

CONCLUSION

Both Deutero–Isaiah and Matthew share a theological insight into the role of Yhwh in shaping the destiny of Israel in herself and in relation to the nations. In Isaiah, Yhwh is depicted as standing outside created time and capable of granting many generations of life to a recipient. Matthew, as I have argued, is caught up in speculation about the *kyklos*, circle, that can be considered to have neither beginning nor end.[13] Matthew sees that life being made available in the εκκλησια (k-k-l-s being its shared consonantal spine with κυκλος), the church. Both texts function as poetic bearers of a message concerning the Servant(s) of this same Yhwh. Again, this does not exhaust the extent of Matthew's exploration of the Servant poems. Several themes, having nothing directly to do with the Name Yhwh, are shared between the poems and the Sermon on the Mount. But that is part of another discussion.

---

13. Kiley, "Matthew's Pi," 1–13.

Without a Wedding Garment: A Note on Matthew 22:12

IRRATIONAL BORDERING ON BIZARRE. Someone dragooned off the streets to come to a feast only to be upbraided for his couture by the royal host and ejected. Nevertheless, there is a reason for the seeming madness at this point in Matthew. I would turn our gaze to Galatians 3:26–28.

> As many of you as were baptized into Christ have clothed yourselves in Christ. For there is neither Jew nor Greek, neither slave nor free and there is not male and female. For you are all one in Christ Jesus.

Have these terms appeared earlier in the text? Not exactly as such but the Evangelist does give us a plausible narrative paraphrase of the Pauline assertion.

NEITHER JEW NOR GREEK:

It is a fact that the Matthean Jesus says "Go nowhere among the Gentiles but go only to the lost sheep of the house of Israel." (10:5, 6). However, that stands in some tension with the culminating great commission of the risen Jesus in chapter 28: "Teach all nations." As for the Pauline formula, Ioudaios occurs a handful of times but *Greek* is nowhere to be found. Instead, the letters of ἔθνος/people are strewn throughout the posted number of those fed in two separate crowds and the resultant overflow of morsels:

²⁰ ἔφαγον ... ἐχορτάσθησαν ... τὸ περισσεῦον [Matt 14:20 and 15:37].

NEITHER SLAVE NOR FREE

Whereas in Matthew 8:8 the παῖς [meaning both slave and child] receives the healing effects of the word of Jesus, and many from east and west are seen as coming to Abraham's banquet, the υἱοὶ/ sons of the reign are given a stern warning about their possible (self-)exclusion from the party.

AND THERE IS NOT MALE AND FEMALE

Matthew's Jesus does not deny the liceity in prior tradition of a Jewish man's right to divorce his wife. Indeed, he defends divorce exacted for reasons of πορνεία, variously understood as sexual immorality or consanguinity (Matt 19:9). However, he also attributes the impulse-to-divorce to hardness of heart and ignorance of the creative Sovereign's positive attitude toward male and female becoming one flesh. Matthew's Jesus even gives clear approbation to the life of the sexually inactive (19:10–12) who make themselves so for the sake of God's reign. This snapshot of the Matthean gender-reveal depicts a landscape neither for the simple-minded given to sloganeering nor for the pastorally insensitive.

The Evangelist has cast the Pauline formula available to him in terms that are plausible within the lifetime of the historical Jesus and that function as proleptic appearance of social categories being relativized in Christ in Matthew's time. Such a reading makes sense of the otherwise difficult attribution of fault to the wedding guest. The speechless guest is someone who, in proximate Pauline terms, could have clothed himself in the appropriate and relativized social relations of the Jesus movement and did not.

WITHOUT A WEDDING GARMENT: A NOTE ON MATTHEW 22:12

What is the relationship of this proposed garment ethic to the behavior of the murderous royal wedding planner who inhabits the parable? Perhaps only this—that the novelty of the inbreaking reign of God in Jesus emerges, improbably, from the shell of a world grown old.

Skylla, Charybdis, and Planktae in Mark 5—7

FOR SEVERAL DECADES NOW, pop culture has portrayed Jesus' walk on the water in all four Gospels as akin to the action of a sailor.[1] The initial point of this note is to emphasize that the maritime episode in Mark 6:45–52 is framed by Mark's allusion to the twin dangers of rock and whirlpool that are present between the coasts of Italy and Sicily. In Homer's *Odyssey*, antiquity's first Greek Bible, the exploits of Odysseus and his crew occur against the backstory that many ships were consigned to a watery grave in those environs. Mark's adaptation in Mark 5–7 is straightforward, though not blatantly obvious. The name of Skylla the sea monster is approximated in this lament:

Ἡ θυγάτηρ σου ἀπέθανεν· τί ἔτι σκύλλεις τὸν διδάσκαλον
Your daughter has died. Why bother the teacher any further? (Mark 5:35).

The letters of her name Skylla are also intercalated in Mark 5:38—

εἰς . . . καὶ . . . θόρυβον . . . κλαίοντας . . . ἀλαλάζοντας.

This Markan verse reporting on the tumult and wailing of a death scene has its analogue in *Odyssey* 12.85 that discusses Skylla

---

1. "Suzanne," lyrics by Leonard Cohen.

making terrible noise i.e. howling (Σκυλλη ναιει δεινον λελακυια) in the cave of the rock where she dwells. This section of the Odyssey portrays the monster using her many heads to devour sailors caught in her tentacles. It is hardly a stretch to hear the concluding grace note of Jesus about the raised girl "Give her something to eat" (Mark 5:43) as the reversal of the monster's agenda.[2]

The letters of Χαρύβδις occur in correct order in Isa 29:13 LXX as quoted in Mark 7: 6, 7—

⁶χείλεσίν . . . τιμᾷ, . . . καρδία αὐτῶν ⁷ . . . σέβονταί . . .διδ ἀσκοντες.

The probability that Charybdis is indeed an organizing principle in this part of Mark is apparent in that the catalogue of vices in Mark 7: 21–23 is instantiated in miniature in the ancient metaphorical expression of calling someone a Charybdis, that is, a whirlpool, of greed.[3]

In between chapters 5 and 7, Mark has placed the rejection of Jesus at Nazareth, the possibility that his disciples will be treated similarly, and the execution of John the Baptizer in prison.

In 7:31–33, the text presents a roundabout itinerary of Jesus [the proximate equivalent of a trip from Vancouver to Atlanta by way of Anchorage]. The Evangelist may have consciously embedded the letters πλαγκταὶ πέτραι/wandering rocks in these verses in order to elicit memory of *Odyssey* 12.60–80 in which sailors are crushed unaware when attempting passage through a narrow strait of rocks and roaring waves. If so, the κήρ—component of ἐκήρυσσον/they announced in Mark 7:36 would in part echo the Homeric Greek words for wax, κηρός—remember Jason and the

---

2. The parallel text in Matthew 9:25, 26 lacks any reference to feeding the girl.

3. See Χαρύβδιν ἁρπαγῆς Aristophanes, *The Knights*, line 248; See Henderson, *Acharnians*. *Knights* 262. The Chorus is speaking about the Paphlagonian. Matthew's parallel text in Matthew 15 lacks any mention of greed as such, though theft is cited in Matt 15:19. However, the thesis that Matthew intends to echo the Markan maritime agenda is rendered relatively improbable by the six-chapter spread (Matthew 9 and 15) in which the possible parallels appear. Luke has no equivalent to the discussion of Isaiah and the vices.

Argonauts—and death/ Κήρ. When considered against that ancient mythological background, the opening of the man's ears (Mark 7:34, 35) limns the maintenance of a safe passage through a dangerous strait. But the end is not yet. Mark is not just repeating an ancient story about avoiding danger. In Mark 8:31–38, Peter tries to dissuade Jesus from his chosen course toward death and Jesus makes the first announcement of his death- and—resurrection.

The reminders of animus and mortality in Mark 5:3—7:30 are interwoven with Mark's good news of restoring a dead girl to life, feeding thousands with a handful of bread and fish, Jesus' walking on water uttering the divine self-predication I AM, and healing many of the sick in Genessaret. So too the epic undertones of death in Mark 7:31–37 prepare indirectly for the text's *peripeteia* announcing death and resurrection in Mark 8. The good news so depicted has foundations intersecting with grave Greco-Roman concerns that make the good news of Jesus welcome in the first place.

A final technical note: While Homer presents the Planktae as an *alternative* route to Ithaka, his poetic successor Apollonius of Rhodes (3rd c BCE) depicts them as *beyond* the region of Skylla and Charybdis. Perhaps we should not be surprised to see that the profile of the Planktae in Mark 7:31–33 follows that of Charybdis in Mark 7:21–23.[4]

---

4. Apollonius, *The Argonautica*, 4.783–90. See Race. *Apollonius*, 392–93.

K-L-B in Mark 7

WHEN JESUS SPEAKS OF the polluting detritus of the heart in Mark 7:14–23, it is not immediately apparent that such a concern is related to the narrative of a persistent Syrophoenician woman arguing for her child in 7:24–30. However, their juxtaposition is no accident and the key to their unity resides in the Hebrew letters בלב.

HEART MATTERS

Vocalic pointing of כלב allows for "as a heart" kĕlēb or "whole heart" kālleb

"Foods cannot cheapen a person, they do not enter the heart, but the stomach; . . . . . . It is from the interior, from the heart of a person, that evil inclinations proceed that cheapen the person" (Mark 7:14–23, especially 19–21).

This ostensible possibility of a Hebrew background is interesting but by itself would have little significance. However, the following narrative emphasizes another entry point into Hebrew and into the Pentateuchal narratives of the reconnoitering of Canaan.

LIKE A DOG

In Mark 7:24–30 the retort of Jesus to the persistent mother implicitly compares her to a dog (keleb).

> 24 From there he set out and went away to the region of Tyre. He entered a house and did not want anyone to know he was there. Yet he could not escape notice, 25 but a woman whose little daughter had an unclean spirit immediately heard about him, and she came and bowed down at his feet. 26 Now the woman was a Gentile, of Syrophoenician origin. She begged him to cast the demon out of her daughter. 27 He said to her, "Let the children be fed first, for it is not fair to take the children's food and throw it to the dogs." 28 But she answered him, "Sir, even the dogs under the table eat the children's crumbs." 29 Then he said to her, "For saying that, you may go—the demon has left your daughter." 30 So she went home, found the child lying on the bed, and the demon gone.

While the retort of Jesus to the persistent mother implicitly compares her to a dog (keleb), those same consonants when pointed as kālēb constitute the name Caleb who in Numbers 13:30 and 14:24 is adamant that the land they have been promised is filled with threat but attainable. He has a "different spirit (from others who are more timorous) and followed Yahweh fully."

It is not much of a stretch to see that bravado is part of the profile of both the mother and Caleb.

Jesus may be recognizing this "dog" as an ally-in-faith in the spirit of Caleb of old. Perhaps the claims in Joshua 15:16–17 and Judges 1:12–13 that Caleb had a daughter played a role in the tradition relaying this story in Mark 7. It is an interesting option but not necessary to detection of the link between keleb/dog and Kaleb as bold pioneer.[1]

Lest there be any doubt that k-l-b is a hidden hand shaping part of Mark 7:14–30, we remember that the chapter begins with

---

1. The church father Origen of Alexandria (ca. 184–263 CE) engages in just such a dual reading of Caleb "as a heart" in his Homilies on Joshua 18.2,3. See Franke, *Joshua, Judges*, 276–77.

K-L-B IN MARK 7

attention not only to washing and eating food but washing utensils as well (Mark 7:4). Nestled in the midst of the Hebrew lexicon's attention to k-l-b is the presence of the word for utensil/vessel, kĕlîy. Any account of organizing principles in Mark 7:1–30, perhaps generated among synagogal homilists, would have to include Hebrew k-l-b.

"...And having spit..." (Mark 7:33 and 8:23)

THIS DAILY DOUBLE WAS short-lived in the Synoptic world. The parallels in Matthew and Luke have been sanitized but what they gained in hygiene they lost in Markan narrative cogency. My suggestion regarding the latter may be stated succinctly. The spit in chapter 7 resumes a theme at the baptism of Jesus, and that in chapter 8 limns the Hebrew for *existence*, thereby anticipating a modulation of Exodus 3 at the Transfiguration.

The baptism in Mark 1 and the healing of the deaf mute in Mark 7 share a portrait of liquid, an opening, and hearing. The letters of ἐβαπτίσθη/he was baptized in Mark 1:9 are sprinkled in the correct order throughout Mark 7:32–34.

³² χεῖρα. ³³ ἀπολαβόμενος αὐτὸν ἀπὸ τοῦ ἰδίαν τοὺς, ³⁴ Εφφαθα, Διανοίχθητι·

The healing of the blind man near Bethsaida in Mark 8 creates a flagstone path on which one moves from implied Hebrew yāraq/spit to its lexical neighbor yēš/existence to the question of Jesus "Who do people say that I am"? We know that we are dealing with Hebrew yēš because Jesus spits eis/into the man's eyes (8:23). Really? Spit into the man's eyes? Yes. Mark chose an expression that approximates Hebrew yēš.[1] The sight gradually restored in

---

1. There will be a similar appeal to Hebrew in the wordplay of Mark 9:47,

"...AND HAVING SPIT..." (MARK 7:33 AND 8:23)

Mark 8 prepares for a vision in Mark 9 of divine glory in which Jesus participates, radiating the presence of I am, now implicitly capitalized I AM (see Exod 3:14). The letters of the phrase ἐγώ εἰμι/I AM are intercalated in Mark 9:3, 4 as is the case with βάτος/ bush in Mark 9:3 (see Exod 3:2). Chapters eight and nine truly work together in this regard in that the letters of μετεμορφώθη/he was transformed are sprinkled throughout Mark 8:23–26—

²³ ἐπιλαβόμενος τῆς χειρὸς κώμης... ὄμματα... ²⁵...χεῖρ ας... ὀφθαλμοὺς...τηλαυγῶς... ²⁶ εἰσέλθῃς.

It will not be lost on the attentive reader that the gradual discernment of the presence of the letters of μετεμορφώθη/he was transformed approximates the man's report that his return to sight happened only gradually (Mark 8:24, 25).

The explicit voice of the Father bookends these exercises from Mark 1–9. The spit in the healings of chapters seven and eight functions allusively to emphasize first the water of the Spirit's creation, then the I AM at work in the Paschal Mystery of Jesus.

"Held together with spit" indicates pure derision in other settings; not in Mark's good news.

49; mālaḥ/salt and mālak reign.

Where and what is Dalmanoutha? (Mark 8:10)

NEITHER ANCIENT MANUSCRIPTS NOR modern excavations have identified a particular site as Dalmanoutha.

HEREWITH TWO SUGGESTIONS, BOTH DEPENDENT ON THE CENTRAL IMPORTANCE OF RENDERING MANOU IN DALMANOUTHA AS DERIVED FROM HEBREW MAN-HU, WHAT IS IT?

1) The first suggestion is predicated on the intersection of the portrait of Jesus with manna.

When the people of Israel saw it, they said to one another "what is it?" for they did not know what it was. And Moses said to them "It is the bread that the Lord has given you to eat" (Exod 16:15). The regulations of the desert wandering in Exodus 16 stipulate that people in the desert are to gather in the morning the manna sufficient for one day (Exod 16:12). That pattern is to hold until the sixth day, when Yhwh gives a double portion of manna so that the people may rest and not collect manna on the Sabbath (Exod 16:22–30).

Now consider the diction of Mark 8:10—"They came to the region of Dalmanoutha." A retroversion from Greek to Aramaic

Where and what is Dalmanoutha? (Mark 8:10)

suggests "They came to the region *of that which pertains to the manna.*"[1] Where is the region that pertains to the manna? Perhaps Mark 1:35–37 offers a clue. There Jesus goes alone to the ἔρημος/ desert to pray *very early in the morning*. Ερημο—all but the case- letter ending s of ἔρημος/ desert, is part of the phrase in 8:10 εις το μερη Δαλμανουθα

At Mark 1:38, we find the letters of μαννα intercalated in Jesus' words—-

³⁸ Ἄγωμεν ἀλλαχοῦ... ἐχομένας...ἵνα

The same verse also provides a transliteration of the sound of the Hebrew mān-hû', the rough breathing of ἵνα providing the h-sound——

Ἄγωμεν ἀλλαχοῦ... ἐχομένας... ἵνα... κηρύξω.

The more extensive portrait of Mark's Jesus is also shaped by this concern for manna. As the manna of Exodus 16 is not collected/gathered on the Sabbath so as to provide for a day of rest, so too in Mark 6:1–6 in the synagogue (linguistically a place of collecting/gathering), Jesus is rejected on a Sabbath, a day of rest. The double dispensation of manna on the sixth day allowing for both feeding and rest on the morrow has its analogue in Mark as well. Jesus states his concern to provide the disciples with rest (Mark 6:31, immediately prior to feeding a crowd). Mark 8 presents another feeding. Note that the word for sixth ἕκτῃ is intercalated into the opening of the second feeding at Mark 8—'Ἐν ἐκείναις ταῖς ἡμέραις—. In both feedings, there is plenty of bread left over. At one level, the people of Mark 1 and 6—8 are walking through the pattern of life narrated by Exodus 16. Mark 1:35–37 announces the subtheme of the manna. Then come the Sabbath rejection and double feedings with bread to spare.

The order of these events—synagogal failure to collect the bread that Jesus is, followed by feedings—corresponds to an aspect

---

1. Marcus *Mark 1–8*, 498 goes so far as to render "which pertains to the region of" but concludes only that Mark places the region on the western...shore of the lake.

of the Hebrew that is read right to left, here in the narrative at large, back to front.

The μαννα-series begun in Mark 1 culminates in 8:10 with Dalmanoutha, encapsulating the subtheme of manna just below the surface of the Markan narrative. Indeed, one may read the letters of the phrase τα μερη Δαλμανουθα intercalated in Mark 1:35–39.

^{35} ἀναστὰς ... ἔρημον ... κἀκεῖ προσηύχετο. ^{36} ... κατεδίωξεν αὐτὸν ^{37} ... λέγουσιν Ἄγωμεν ··· ἐχομένας ἵνα ... τοῦτο ...] ἐξῆλθον. ^{39} καὶ

Note also the pun in which the ψιχιων/ crumbs of Jesus (7:28) communicate his life/ ψυχην (10:4, 5).

This identification of Jesus as manna derived from Exodus 16 works in tandem with aspects of prophetic vision. Amos 8:11, 12 describes a famine and a search—ζητουσιν——for the word of the Lord. That sort of famine is distinct from a hunger for bread, says Amos. Hence, everyone is searching [ζητουσιν] for Mark's Jesus in 1:37 who sees his task as preaching (1:38).

The early morning prayer at Mark 1:35 reflects the similar portrait of Yhwh's servant at Isaiah 50:4 "Morning by morning he wakens, he wakens my ear to hear as those who are taught." Note also how carefully the awakening of the ear *morning by morning* reflects the diction of Exodus 16:21 They gathered the manna morning by morning πρωι πρωι.

This multifaceted vision of Jesus, crafted in a concentrated space, anticipates the even more thoroughly developed Bread of Life discourse in John 6 where Jesus is both bread from heaven and the one whose words are spirit and life.

2) The second suggestion emphasizes the role of God's reign in the presentation of Jesus as manna.

Note the word immediately preceding Dalmanoutha, that is, μερη, region. One Semitic background to μερη Δαλμανουθα would be *mirdāh l' manoutha* dominion of the manna.

Where and what is Dalmanoutha? (Mark 8:10)

That rendering would not only respect the Hebrew basis of Exodus 16 and 17 but also the emergent theme of the reign of God in Mark 1-8.

The gift of his body and blood via the sign of bread and wine in Mark 14 and under the titular sign of his sovereignty at the cross in Mark 15 bring this theme of *manna* to its conclusion in the Gospel. Look for the italicized letters μάννα in each of the following verses, Mark 14:22, 23 and Mark 15:26, 27—

Mark 14—

σῶμά [23]...λαβὼν ποτήριον εὐχαριστήσας
Take, this is my body. And taking a cup, having given thanks......

and Mark 15

[26] ἐπιγεγραμμένη·... βασιλεὺς τῶν Ἰουδαίων. [27] καὶ
And the inscription of the charge against him read, The king of the Jews. And......

CONCLUDING OBSERVATIONS

Lest 1:35 seem a little late in the narrative to be introducing such an important leitmotif of the text, consider the question in Mark 1:27 "What is this?" whose Hebrew version mah—zeh is a near analogue to mān-hû'. The gradual, not instantaneous, granting of sight in Mark 8:22—26 serves as exemplar of a vision to which the Evangelist gives gradual access.

A final word about the geographical location of the site in Mark 8:10. Mark 7:31 places Jesus at the Sea of Galilee. Mark 1:21 places him in Capernaum (on the north shore of the Lake of Galilee). Together, they bookend the Evangelist's portrait of the manna in the first half of the text.

In sum, Dalmanoutha is a deserted region near the north end of the Sea of Galilee, perhaps near Capernaum, the same or like that in Mark 1:35-37, where Jesus functions both as bread and word of God.

Job 29 in Mark 9:1–29

THE TEXT OF JOB 29 provides part of the skeletal structure of that point in the Markan narrative when his cross and resurrection are coming more fully into view. In so doing, the Joban chapter says something about who Jesus is.

In chapter 29, Job speaks of his former days in terms that will populate the Markan Transfiguration and ensuing exorcism:[1]

Light: by God's light I walked through darkness (vs. 3)[2]

Tent: I was in my autumn days when the friendship of God was upon my tent (vs.4)[3]

Silence: The princes refrained from talking and laid their hand on their mouth (vs. 9)[4]

Prey: I broke the fangs of the unrighteous and made him drop his prey from his teeth (vs. 17)[5]

---

1. First renderings are those of the *Revised Standard Version*.

2. "When I could walk by its (God's) light in the dark." Greenstein, *Job*, 122.

3. "Just as I'd been in my earlier days, when my tent stood under Eloah's bond." Greenstein, *Job*, 122.

4. "Princes would hold back their words, placing a hand over their mouth" Greenstein, *Job*, 122.

5. Mark slightly modulates this Joban statement when he says that the paroxysms imposed on the child include the grinding of his teeth (Mark 9:18). "I would break the fangs of the depraved and cast the prey out of his teeth."

And from Mark 9 we hear of
Jesus in his brilliance (vs. 3)
Peter and his babble about tents (vs. 5)[6]
Jesus enjoining temporary silence about this vision (vs. 9)
And Jesus [said] 'You mute and deaf spirit, I order you, leave him and no longer enter him' (vs. 25)

The father's request for βοήθησ-/help in Mark 9:22 reflects the same verb in the same sense as in Job 29:12 LXX. The statement in Job 29:16 LXX "I was a father to the powerless" is given ample explication in the several verses of this Markan text devoted to the question of God's power and human impotence when confronted with especially malevolent spirits (Mark 9:22-23, 28-29).

This pericope contains an implicit statement about the humanity of Jesus, crafted partially along the lines of Job Everyman. In both sets of texts, the speakers are approaching the culmination of their trouble and the definitive divine speech that transforms it. Mark also recognizes the humanity of Jesus in a way that gives wide berth to the power of God inherent in him. Indeed, Jesus acting as father on behalf of a powerless son in this narrative (Mark 9:14-29) is certainly intended to be seen in light of his identity as Son to the Father in the previous pericope (Mark 9:1-13).

Greenstein, *Job*, 123.

6. Mark's Greek σκηνάς/tents reflects Hebrew אָהֳלִי/ āhŏlî in the Masoretic text of Job 29: 4. The Septuagint of Job 29:4 does not read *tents* but rather it reads οικου/ house. The letters of οικοι/houses are strewn in the correct order throughout Peter's statement in Mark 9:5 ποιήσωμεν...σκηνάς σοὶ.

Subtext and Intertext in Mark 16:1—8

THE ALLURE OF THE last eight verses of the Gospel of Mark continues unabated in recent scholarship.[1] The purpose of this study is to draw the discourse about Mark 16:1–8 into contact with

- The Greek rhetorical exercise of *aposiopēsis*
- individual letters of the word for letter, *gramma,* within Mark 16:1
- new aspects of Psalms already presented in the body of Mark 1–15
- aspects of Exodus 16 such as *manna* in Mark 16:1–8
- theophany to Elijah (1 Kings 19:12) in Mark 16
- roots in Pauline theology
- intercalated Alleluia and the Pindaric Victory Ode

What these exercises have in common is attention to letters that form intelligible words among words, not only discrete words

---

1. For example, nearly one dozen peer-reviewed essays exploring Mark 16 during the years 2018–2023 were placed in a virtual environment under the direction of Claire Clivaz and with the financial assistance of the Swiss National Science Foundation.

as such. As such, the Markan author is engaged in a process that is to some extent hidden.

APOSIOPĒSIS

As far as it goes, there is nothing wrong with the observation that the empty tomb's linen-clad figure and the women's silence have a proximate analogue in the linen-clad figure in Dan 12:6 and his assertion that the words of his revelation are shut up and sealed until the time of the end (Dan 12:9). However, the Greek rhetorical term *aposiopēsis* offers a complementary parallel to that in Daniel. *Aposiopēsis* means both a *falling silence* as well as *breaking off in mid-sentence*. An example resides in Demosthenes *Orations* 23.1 *On the Crown*:

> 'I could on my part—but I do not want to say anything offensive at the beginning of my speech' (ἀλλ' ἐμοὶ μὲν—οὐ βούλομαι δὲ δυσχερὲς οὐδὲν εἰπεῖν ἀρχόμενος τοῦ λόγου). 21.[2]

See also the description of Alexander's friends who, aggrieved at his silence, forced their way in δείσαντες οἱ φίλοι τὴν ἀποσιώπησιν εἰσῆλθον βίᾳ.[3]

I cite the rhetorical figure here because the letters constituting ἀποσιώπησις/aposiopēsis exist within Mark 16:7, 8, stretching from αὐτοῦ to ἔκστασις—

> 7 ἀλλὰ ὑπάγετε εἴπατε τοῖς μαθηταῖς αὐτοῦ καὶ τῷ Πέτρῳ ὅτι Προάγει ὑμᾶς εἰς τὴν Γαλιλαίαν·
> ἐκεῖ αὐτὸν ὄψεσθε, καθὼς εἶπεν ὑμῖν. 8 καὶ ἐξελθοῦσαι ἔφυγον ἀπὸ τοῦ μνημείου, εἶχεν]γὰρ
> αὐτὰς τρόμος καὶ ἔκστασις· καὶ οὐδενὶ οὐδὲν εἶπαν, ἐφοβοῦντο γάρ.

---

[2]. Cited in Kim, *Figures of Silence*, 32–49.
[3]. Plutarch, *Parallel Lives*, Alexander 52.1. See Perrin, *Plutarch*, 374–75.

This observation is unremarkable by itself. However, this subtext of Mark 16:7, 8 is immediately followed by clauses that illustrate the two meanings of the word:
They said nothing to anyone
and
They feared for...

It has been a half century since Pieter W. van der Horst asked whether a book can end with gar.[4] To the best of my knowledge, the tight juxtaposition between figure and illustration, ἀποσιώπησις and example, has not been considered in that endeavor. That oversight, such as it is, is due to inattention to subtext composed of letters forming words among words.

GRAMMA/LETTER WITHIN MARK 16:1

The letters γράμμα are sprinkled, intercalated if you wish, into the opening of the chapter, beginning at διαγενομένου and ending with Μαρία:

διαγενομένου... Μαρία... Μαγδαληνὴ... Μαρία

This is not the only intercalated word present here, as we shall soon see, but it announces up front the grammatical agenda operative in the pericope.

NEW ASPECTS OF PSALMS ALREADY PRESENTED IN MARK 1–15

I cite here some of the ways in which Psalms 2, 22, 110 and 118 affect the empty tomb narrative. Each of these Psalms has been presented earlier in Mark:

---

4. Van der Horst "Can a book end with gar?" 121–24. Other research on vss. 7, 8 includes Knox "The Ending of St. Mark's Gospel" 13–23; Harris, "On the Alternative Ending" 96–103; Iverson, "A Further Word" 7–94; Aernie "Cruciform Discipleship" 779–97; Lincoln, "The Promise and the Failure" 283–300.

Subtext and Intertext in Mark 16:1—8

Psalm 2 in Mark 1; Psalm 22 in Mark 15; Psalm 110 in Mark 12; Psalm 118 in Mark 11. Some commentators are unwilling to say that Psalm 2 is quoted in Mark 1:11 "You are my son." However, the adjacent grouping of the titles Christ and Son in Mark 1:1, also present in Psalm 2, make it likely that the Psalm as such is in view. Psalm 22:1 "My God, my God, why have you abandoned me?" is presented in Mark 15:34. Psalm 110:1 "The Sovereign said to my sovereign 'Sit at my right hand until I make your enemies your footstool'" is presented in Mark 12:36. Finally, Psalm 118:25, 26 "Blessed be the one coming in the name of the Sovereign" is quoted at Mark 11:9.

In what follows, I present the Markan verses seriatim, verses 1–8, and the Psalms in their Septuagintal form that seem to affect them.

Mark 16:1

Καὶ διαγενομένου τοῦ σαββάτου Μαρία ἡ Μαγδαληνὴ καὶ Μαρία ἡ τοῦ Ἰακώβου καὶ Σαλώμη ἠγόρασαν ἀρώματα ἵνα ἐλθοῦσαι ἀλείψωσιν αὐτόν.

And when the Sabbath was over, Mary Magdalene and Mary the Mother of James and Salome bought spices in order that they might go and anoint him.

From Psalm 2:12 LXX the verse draws the word μακάριος/blessed, happy, beginning with Markan διαγενομένου and ending with ἐλθοῦσαι. This list of persons partially overlaps with that in Mark 15:40, 47 in which the word μακάριος/blessed is also intercalated. The lists of women visiting the tomb in the other Synoptic Gospels do not admit of this construal.

From Psalm 21:23, 26 LXX the Markan verse draws ἐκκλησία/congregation, beginning with Markan διαγενομένου and ending with ἵνα. This is also true of the list of women in Mark 15:40 beginning with δὲ and ending with Σαλώμη. From Psalm 21:29 LXX the evangelist draws βασιλεία/reign, sovereignty beginning with

33

σαββάτου and ending with αὐτόν. The intercalary traffic goes in the other direction as well. The name Μαρία in Mark is also present amid the letters of Psalm 21:10 LXX.

From Psalm 117 LXX the evangelist draws the Psalm's frequently repeated ἔλεος/mercy, beginning with διαγενομένου and ending with ἐλθοῦσαι.

Mark 16:2

> καὶ λίαν πρωΐ ᾗ μιᾷ τῶν σαββάτων ἔρχονται ἐπὶ τὸ μνημεῖον ἀνατείλαντος τοῦ ἡλίου.
> And very early on the first day of the week they went to the tomb when the sun had risen.

Psalm 109:3, 4 LXX contains the sprinkled letters of λίαν πρωΐ/very early. Similarly, Psalm 109: 3, 4 LXX contain the sprinkled letters of ἀνατελλ-, the root of ἀνατείλαντος/rise.

Psalm 117 LXX's frequently chanted ἔλεος/mercy is present in this Markan verse as well, beginning with ἔρχονται and ending with ἀνατείλαντος.

Mark 16:3

> καὶ ἔλεγον πρὸς ἑαυτάς· Τίς ἀποκυλίσει ἡμῖν τὸν λίθον ἐκ τῆς θύρας τοῦ μνημείου;
> And they said to each other "Who will roll away the stone from the door of the tomb for us?"

The phrase of Psalm 117:22 LXX stone, head of the corner/cornerstone begins with λίθος/stone that is present in this Markan verse. The word γωνίας/of the corner is present here in Mark, beginning with ἔλεγον and ending with ἀποκυλίσει.

The presence of that Psalm's ἔλεος/mercy is also registered here, beginning with ἔλεγον and ending with πρός and yet again beginning with ἑαυτάς and ending with θύρας.

Subtext and Intertext in Mark 16:1—8

The evangelist names a θύρα/door in this verse. That term is intercalated in Psalm 117:19, 20 LXX.

Mark 16:4

καὶ ἀναβλέψασαι θεωροῦσιν ὅτι ἀποκεκύλισται ὁ λίθος, ἦν γὰρ μέγας σφόδρα.
And looking up they saw that the stone was rolled back—it was very large.

The κεφα of Psalm 117: 22 LXX's κεφαλή is present in this Markan verse, beginning with ἀποκεκύλισται and ending with σφόδρα.

Beginning with the ε of μνημείου in verse 3, the word for mercy is present in this verse as well, continuing through ἀναβλέψασαι and ending in θεωροῦσιν.

Mark 16:5

καὶ εἰσελθοῦσαι εἰς τὸ μνημεῖον εἶδον νεανίσκον καθήμενον ἐν τοῖς δεξιοῖς περιβεβλημένον στολὴν λευκήν, καὶ ἐξεθαμβήθησαν.
And entering the tomb they saw a youth seated on the right, dressed in a white garment and they were greatly surprised.

On the right, δεξιοῖς, reflects the same word in Psalm 109:1 LXX.[5]

From Psalm 109:3 LXX the evangelist has incorporated the ἐξε of ἐξεγέννησα/I have begotten in the word ἐξεθαμβήθησαν.

The letters of the evangelist's νεανίσκον are also present in Psalm 109:5, 6 LXX.

The final letters λή of the κεφαλή/head of the corner Psalm 117:22 LXX are present in the εἰσελθοῦσαι and μνημεῖον of this Markan verse. Note that the evangelist has placed the phrase cornerstone/head of the corner (Mark 16:3—5) in such a way that it concludes at the approximate halfway point of the pericope. The

---

5. As noted by Collins, *Mark: A Commentary*, 795.

narrative will turn the corner in a sense in the next verse when the youth begins to speak.

Ἔλεος/mercy of Psalm 117 LXX is present in Mark, beginning with εἰσελθοῦσαι and ending with νεανίσκον.

Mark 16:6

ὁ δὲ λέγει αὐταῖς· Μὴ ἐκθαμβεῖσθε· Ἰησοῦν ζητεῖτε τὸν Ναζαρηνὸν τὸν ἐσταυρωμένον· ἠγέρθη, οὐκ ἔστιν ὧδε· ἴδε ὁ τόπος ὅπου ἔθηκαν αὐτόν·
And he said to them "Do not be amazed; you seek Jesus the Nazarene, the crucified. He has been raised. He is not here; look at the place where they laid him.

The explicit ἐσταυρωμένον/crucified here is present by intercalation in Psalm 21:15 LXX. The verb ἀναγγέλλ/announce in Psalm 21:32 LXX begins to be present here in Mark, starting with ἔθηκαν αὐτόν. It will be completed in Mark 16:7.

The -γέννησα, completing the ἐξεγέννησα/I have begotten of Psalm 109:3 LXX, is present here in Mark, beginning with λέγει and ending with ἐσταυρωμένον.

The explicit ἠγέρθη/he has been raised in this verse is present in intercalation in Psalm 117:21—23 LXX.

This Markan verse contains the letters of δικαιοσύνη/righteousness, justice that are present also in Psalm 117:19 LXX.

Ἔλεος/mercy of Psalm 117 LXX is present here in Mark, beginning with δὲ and ending with ἐσταυρωμένον·.

Mark 16:7

ἀλλὰ ὑπάγετε εἴπατε τοῖς μαθηταῖς αὐτοῦ καὶ τῷ Πέτρῳ ὅτι Προάγει ὑμᾶς εἰς τὴν Γαλιλαίαν· ἐκεῖ αὐτὸν ὄψεσθε, καθὼς εἶπεν ὑμῖν.
But go, tell his disciples and Peter to go to Galilee; there you will see him, just as he told you.

Subtext and Intertext in Mark 16:1—8

-Ἄγγελλ, the completion of the word in Psalm 21:32 LXX ἀναγγέλλ/ announce occurs in this Markan verse, beginning at ἀλλὰ and ending at Γαλιλαίαν. Similarly, ἐποίησεν/done from the same Psalmic verse is begun in the intercalated ἐπ of εἶπεν and will be completed in Mark 16:8. The phrase in Psalm 21:26 LXX εὐχας μου begins to be present at the end of this Markan verse, at εἶπεν ὑμῖν and will be completed in Mark 16:8.

Psalm 109:7 LXX uses the verb ὑψώσει/he will lift, a verb intercalated throughout the end of Mark 16:7 among the words αὐτὸν ὄψεσθε, καθὼς εἶπεν. This seventh Markan verse also sprinkles the initial letters for Morningstar ἑωσφόρος within the words ὄψεσθε, καθὼς. That Morningstar will be completed in Mark 16:8.

The ἔλεος /mercy of Psalm 117 LXX begins in this Markan verse with εἰς and ends with ὄψεσθε. The evangelist names Πέτρος here. The letters of the name are also sprinkled throughout Psalm 117:22-23 LXX.

Mark 16:8

καὶ ἐξελθοῦσαι ἔφυγον ἀπὸ τοῦ μνημείου, εἶχεν γὰρ αὐτὰς τρόμος καὶ ἔκστασις· καὶ οὐδενὶ οὐδὲν εἶπαν, ἐφοβοῦντο γάρ

And going out, they fled from the tomb, for terror and astonishment laid hold of them and they said nothing to anyone. They feared for...

τρόμος and φοβ-, terror and fear, while not unique to Psalm 2, do occur there in Psalm 2:10, 11 LXX.

ὀιησεν, the completion of ἐποίησεν/done (Psalm 21:32 LXX) occurs here beginning with ἐξελθοῦσαι and ending with οὐδενί. The letters of the final particle γάρ also occur in Psalm 21:32 LXX. The letters—χας μου, the completion of Psalm 21:26 LXX εὐχας μου occurs in the Markan words εἶχεν γὰρ αὐτὰς τρόμος... οὐδενί.

The κεφα- of κεφαλή (Ps 109:7 LXX) is present here, beginning in ἔκστασις· and ending in the final γάρ. The incomplete articulation of κεφαλή works together with the abrupt nature of the final γάρ to suggest an earlier teaching in the Gospel that no one among humans knows the (time of the appearance of the) Day or the Hour (Mark 13:32).[6] The completion of the word ἑωσφόρος/Morningstar resides in the words ἔφυγον... γὰρ... τρόμος.[7]

The ἔλεος /mercy of Psalm 117 LXX begins in this Markan verse with ἐξελθοῦσαι and ends with αὐτάς.

ASPECTS OF EXODUS 16 IN MARK 16:1–8

The narrative of the empty tomb in Mark is in dialogue with the narrative of the provision of food during the desert journey in Exodus 16.

Early, πρωι, you will be filled with bread (Exodus 16: 12)

They said each to the other τί ἐστιν τοῦτο; "What is this?" (Exodus 16:15).

Compare—-
λίαν πρωΐ /very early (Mark 16:2)
And they said to one another, τί ἐστιν τοῦτο; sprinkled throughout these words of Mark 16:2–4

> Τίς ἀποκυλίσει... τῆς... τοῦ... μνημείου... ἀναβλέψασα ι... ὅτι... ἀποκεκύλισται... ὁ.

The explicitly named subject in Exodus 16:12 is ἄρτος/bread.

---

6. The concluding letters—λή are supplied in both longer endings of the Gospel that emphasize evidence of the resurrection rather than oblique allusions to the Parousia.

7. Taylor, *Gospel*, 604—5 points out the tension between λίαν πρωΐ /very early (Mark 16:2a) and sunrise (Mark 16:2b). Intercalated ἕσπερος ἀστήρ/evening star in Psalm 109:1–3 has its intercalated counterpart in Mark 16:2–4. Furthermore, the bright star of night and equally bright star of morning were even in antiquity suspected to be the same star in a very tight circumpolar orbit. It may be that Mark delineates two times at the boundaries of night and day so that he may allude to Jesus as the one generated in the in-between time, a la Psalm 109 LXX.

Subtext and Intertext in Mark 16:1—8

The inference through intercalation regarding Jesus in Mark 16:6 is that he functions as bread. See the letters of ἄρτος sprinkled throughout

Ναζαρηνὸν τὸν ἐσταυρωμένον.

We probably would not be too far amiss to suggest that this bread persona is forged in the fire of the I AM self-predication previously seen at the burning bush in Exodus 3:14. Within the words of the youth in Mark 16:6, 7 is the intercalated phrase Ἐγώ εἰμι ὁ ὤν/I AM WHO AM——-ἐσταυρωμένον· ἠγέρθη... ὧδε· ἴδε... εἴπατε μαθηταῖς... αὐτοῦ... τῷ... τήν.

THEOPHANY TO ELIJAH IN MARK 16

Wind, fire, and a "still, small voice"; so says the narrative of theophany to Elijah in 1 Kings 19. However, the Greek text of 1 Kgs 19:12 φωνὴ αὔρας λεπτῆς is better rendered as "a sound of a slight breeze." These Greek letters αὔρας λεπτῆς/slight breeze are embedded in the words of the young man in the empty tomb (Mark 16:6, 7). We can see that these same words in proximity to one another also occur in Mark 1:44 but the order is different. The sequence chosen by the Evangelist in Mark 16 allows this precise identification as an echo of the theophany to Elijah. Look for italicized αὔρας λεπτῆς—

⁶ ὁ δὲ λέγει αὐταῖς... Ναζαρηνὸν... ἐσταυρωμένον·...ἔστ ιν ⁷ ἀλλὰ ὑπάγετε εἴπατε μαθηταῖς

This is a natural complement to the Elijah sequence in earlier chapters of Mark: Elijah and wind (Mark 6:15, 48)) and Elijah and fire (Mark 8:28 and 9:22).

ROOTS IN PAULINE THEOLOGY

In 1 Cor 15:4, Paul clearly asserts that Christ was buried and then raised on the third day according to the Scriptures. I would suggest that the intercalated dialogue with the Psalms and Exodus and the theophany to Elijah in Mark 16 are very much a part of that procedure.

What happens in the subtext of the narrative characters at the end of Mark may also be seen as reflected in a theological principle articulated in the letter to the Colossians. One immediately thinks of this verse——

ἀπεθάνετε γάρ, καὶ ἡ ζωὴ ὑμῶν κέκρυπται σὺν τῷ Χριστῷ ἐν τῷ θεῷ·
"You have died, and your life is hidden with Christ in God" (Col 3:3)

Consider the presence of two of these ideas in Mark 16—
Ζωή/life:

Ναζαρηνὸν ἐσταυρωμένον ἠγέρθη (Mark 16:6)

Κρύπτ/hidden—-

καὶ Πέτρῳ ὑμᾶς εἶπεν τοῦ (Mark 16:7, 8)

However, current exegesis frequently places that epistle somewhere in the 80s of the first century CE whereas the Gospel is often seen as a product of the late 60s so in this instance the traffic moves from Mark to Colossians.[8]

Nevertheless, another avenue from Paul to intercalated Mark suggests itself. The undisputed first letter to the Corinthians (a product of the 50s) speaks of God's hidden wisdom in Christ made known to believers through the Spirit (1 Cor 2:7, 8, 12). That may have been a sufficient stimulus for the Markan evangelist to portray not only explicit theologoumena but also subtextual themes as he articulates the Mystery of Jesus crucified and risen, revealed first to what will be called the church.

---

8. Brown, *Introduction to the New Testament*, 615–16, 163–64.

SUBTEXT AND INTERTEXT IN MARK 16:1—8

INTERCALATED ALLELUIA AND THE PINDARIC VICTORY ODE

If Greek superscriptions to the Psalms were available to the evangelist, we may hear a fitting response to the Name in the Ἀλληλουια that begins in the ἀλλὰ of Mark 16:7 and concludes in the initial καὶ of Mark 16:8. Running in tandem with that acclamation is the name of the victory ode celebrated after athletic contests, the ἐπινίκιον. It is present here in Mark 16:7, starting with εἴπατε and ending with αὐτὸν. As in the Pindaric iterations, this Markan facsimile is attentive to the location of the victory:

"See the place where they laid him." (Mark 16:7).[9] At one level, this moment is the fruition of the Evangelist's acclamation of Jesus as thoroughbred in chapter One. Commentators have long recognized that Mark 1:43 presents Jesus making a sound, ἐμβριμησάμενος, like that of a snorting, vibrant horse. Mark complements that portrait in 1:45 with the intercalated letters of the name of the victorious horse, Φερένικος/bearing victory, celebrated in Pindar's first Olympian Ode, line 18. Mark's Jesus runs a very particular kind of steeplechase. Nurtured perhaps by the Pindar scrolls at the Alexandrian Library, the Evangelist populates his Gospel with the rolling thunder of εὐθύς/immediately to good effect.[10]

CONCLUSION

The intercalary *modus operandi* of the Markan evangelist can be traced in some detail as has been shown here, although these observations are not exhaustive.[11] This effort bears bright promise

---

9. The explicit cutting short of a subject as in Mark 16:8 is in fact another of the features of Pindaric *epinicia*. See Hutchinson, *Greek Lyric Poetry*, 368—70. Consider the exercise of ἀποσιώπησις discussed at the beginning of this essay.

10. Noteworthy studies of Pindar, both with extensive bibliographies, include Carne-Ross, *Pindar* and Schmidt, *The First Poets*.

11. In the words of the young man in Mark 16:6 reside the letters of the name of the mortal Τιθωνός/Tithonos beloved of Dawn, who grants him

for a better understanding of other parts of the text as well. Yet no careful readers will be duped into thinking that the Mystery that Mark articulates can thereby be controlled. The sounds of the Markan dawn remain aligned with the One begotten before the Morningstar and one is rendered. . .

---

immortality. Begin reading at αὐταῖς and end with ἔστιν.

Follow the feet (Luke 7:36–50)

LUKE 7:36–50 MENTIONS THE feet of Jesus seven times, more than in any of the near-parallels in the other Synoptics and John. The purpose of this note is to assay a better understanding of the narrative value attached to these several instances of attention to his feet. My thesis is that Luke refers to the feet primarily because of the promise of Gen 3:15, spoken to the serpent:

> There will be enmity between you and the woman,
> And between your seed and her seed,
> He shall bruise your head and
> You shall bruise his heel.

This English rendering reflects the Hebrew for *bruising* head and heel.

However, the Greek reads somewhat differently:

> καὶ ἔχθραν θήσω ἀνὰ μέσον σοῦ καὶ ἀνὰ μέσον τῆς γυναικὸς καὶ ἀνὰ μέσον τοῦ σπέρματός σου καὶ ἀνὰ μέσον τοῦ σπέρματος αὐτῆς· αὐτός σου τηρήσει κεφαλήν, καὶ σὺ τηρήσεις αὐτοῦ πτέρναν.

According to Philo, first century Jewish philosopher and exegete, the latter part of the verse, using τέρειν, offers two possibilities for interpreters—

—guard and keep safely in memory OR *watch closely* to effect destruction.[1]

Thus, a Lukan reading of Genesis 3:15b in Philonic mode reads "you will watch closely his heel (to effect destruction) and he will watch your head closely (to effect destruction)." The full texts are as follows:

[36] Ἠρώτα δέ τις αὐτὸν τῶν Φαρισαίων ἵνα φάγῃ μετ' αὐτοῦ· καὶ εἰσελθὼν εἰς τὸν οἶκον τοῦ Φαρισαίου [κατεκλίθη. [37] καὶ ἰδοὺ γυνὴ] ἥτις ἦν ἐν τῇ πόλει ἁμαρτωλός,] καὶ ἐπιγνοῦσα ὅτι] κατάκειται ἐν τῇ οἰκίᾳ τοῦ Φαρισαίου, κομίσασα ἀλάβαστρον μύρου [38] καὶ στᾶσα] ὀπίσω παρὰ τοὺς πόδας αὐτοῦ κλαίουσα,] τοῖς δάκρυσιν ἤρξατο βρέχειν τοὺς πόδας αὐτοῦ καὶ ταῖς θριξὶν τῆς κεφαλῆς αὐτῆς ἐξέμασσεν, καὶ κατεφίλει τοὺς πόδας αὐτοῦ καὶ ἤλειφεν τῷ μύρῳ. [39] ἰδὼν δὲ ὁ Φαρισαῖος ὁ καλέσας αὐτὸν εἶπεν ἐν ἑαυτῷ λέγων· Οὗτος εἰ] ἦν προφήτης, ἐγίνωσκεν ἂν τίς καὶ ποταπὴ ἡ γυνὴ ἥτις ἅπτεται αὐτοῦ, ὅτι ἁμαρτωλός ἐστιν. [40] καὶ ἀποκριθεὶς ὁ Ἰησοῦς εἶπεν πρὸς αὐτόν· Σίμων, ἔχω σοί τι εἰπεῖν. ὁ δέ·] Διδάσκαλε, εἰπέ, φησίν. [41] δύο χρεοφειλέται ἦσαν δανιστῇ τινι· ὁ εἷς ὤφειλεν δηνάρια πεντακόσια, ὁ δὲ ἕτερος πεντήκοντα. [42] μὴ] ἐχόντων αὐτῶν ἀποδοῦναι ἀμφοτέροις ἐχαρίσατο. τίς οὖν] αὐτῶν πλεῖον] ἀγαπήσει αὐτόν; [43] []ἀποκριθεὶς Σίμων εἶπεν· Ὑπολαμβάνω ὅτι ᾧ τὸ πλεῖον ἐχαρίσατο. ὁ δὲ εἶπεν αὐτῷ· Ὀρθῶς ἔκρινας. [44] καὶ στραφεὶς πρὸς τὴν γυναῖκα τῷ Σίμωνι ἔφη· Βλέπεις ταύτην τὴν γυναῖκα; εἰσῆλθόν σου εἰς τὴν οἰκίαν, ὕδωρ] μοι ἐπὶ] πόδας οὐκ ἔδωκας· αὕτη δὲ τοῖς δάκρυσιν ἔβρεξέν μου τοὺς πόδας καὶ ταῖς []θριξὶν αὐτῆς ἐξέμαξεν. [45] φίλημά μοι οὐκ ἔδωκας· αὕτη δὲ ἀφ' ἧς εἰσῆλθον οὐ διέλιπεν καταφιλοῦσά μου τοὺς πόδας. [46] ἐλαίῳ τὴν κεφαλήν μου οὐκ ἤλειψας· αὕτη δὲ μύρῳ ἤλειψεν τοὺς πόδας μου. [47] οὗ χάριν, λέγω σοι, ἀφέωνται αἱ ἁμαρτίαι αὐτῆς αἱ πολλαί, ὅτι ἠγάπησεν πολύ· ᾧ δὲ ὀλίγον ἀφίεται, ὀλίγον ἀγαπᾷ. [48] εἶπεν δὲ αὐτῇ· Ἀφέωνταί σου αἱ ἁμαρτίαι. [49] καὶ ἤρξαντο οἱ συνανακείμενοι λέγειν ἐν ἑαυτοῖς· Τίς οὗτός ἐστιν ὃς καὶ ἁμαρτίας ἀφίησιν; [50] εἶπεν δὲ πρὸς τὴν γυναῖκα· Ἡ πίστις σου σέσωκέν σε· πορεύου εἰς εἰρήνην.

---

1. Philo, *Allegorical Interpretation of Genesis 2, 3*. Book 3.189. See Colson, *Philo*, 428–31.

Follow the Feet (Luke 7:36–50)

³⁶ *One of the Pharisees asked Jesus to eat with him, and he went into the Pharisee's house and took his place at the table.* ³⁷ *And a woman in the city, who was a sinner, having learned that he was eating in the Pharisee's house, brought an alabaster jar of ointment.* ³⁸ *She stood behind him at his feet, weeping, and began to bathe his feet with her tears and to dry them with her hair. Then she continued kissing his feet and anointing them with the ointment.* ³⁹ *Now when the Pharisee who had invited him saw it, he said to himself, "If this man were a prophet, he would have known who and what kind of woman this is who is touching him—that she is a sinner."* ⁴⁰ *Jesus spoke up and said to him, "Simon, I have something to say to you." "Teacher," he replied, "speak."* ⁴¹ *"A certain creditor had two debtors; one owed five hundred denarii, the other fifty.* ⁴² *When they could not pay, he canceled the debts for both of them. Now which of them will love him more?"* ⁴³ *Simon answered, "I suppose the one for whom he canceled the greater debt." And Jesus said to him, "You have judged rightly."* ⁴⁴ *Then turning toward the woman, he said to Simon, "Do you see this woman? I entered your house; you gave me no water for my feet, but she has bathed my feet with her tears and dried them with her hair.* ⁴⁵ *You gave me no kiss, but from the time I came in she has not stopped kissing my feet.* ⁴⁶ *You did not anoint my head with oil, but she has anointed my feet with ointment.* ⁴⁷ *Therefore, I tell you, her sins, which were many, have been forgiven; hence she has shown great love. But the one to whom little is forgiven, loves little."* ⁴⁸ *Then he said to her, "Your sins are forgiven."* ⁴⁹ *But those who were at the table with him began to say among themselves, "Who is this who even forgives sins?"* ⁵⁰ *And he said to the woman, "Your faith has saved you; go in peace."*

Willingness to recognize Luke's interweaving of the letters of words within the explicitly stated words grounds a case for seeing Genesis 3 as a formative factor in this pericope. For example, ὄφις serpent, in the Greek of Gen 3:1 is firmly embedded in the description of Simon οἶκον . . . Φαρισαίων in Luke 7:36. Presumably, such an assertion is more an example of religious polemic than a fully accurate assessment of the piety of actual Pharisees of the period.[2]

In addition, Jesus trains his attention on Simon's head in 7:41b–42 insofar as each of the letters of κεφαλή/head are present in the words of Jesus.

[41] πεντακόσια δὲ ἀμφοτέροις ἐχαρίσατο. πλεῖον ἀγαπήσει

Moreover, all of the letters of the Greek word for watch τέρειν /watch closely and πτέρνα /heel, the object of the serpent's watching in Genesis 3:15, are scattered throughout the words describing the private thoughts of Simon in Luke 7:39, 40a—

[39] ἰδὼν δὲ ὁ Φαρισαῖος ὁ καλέσας αὐτὸν εἶπεν ἐν ἑαυτῷ λέγων· Οὗτος εἰ ἦν προφήτης, ἐγίνωσκεν ἂν τίς καὶ ποταπὴ ἡ γυνὴ ἥτις ἅπτεται αὐτοῦ, ὅτι ἁμαρτωλός ἐστιν. [40] καὶ
[39] Now when the Pharisee who had invited him saw it, he said to himself, "If this man were a prophet, he would have known who and what kind of woman this is who is touching him—that she is a sinner." [40] And

All of the letters in πτέρνα/heel are present at the crucifixion scene at Skull Hill in Luke 23:33, 34b and all of the letters in τέρειν/watch, are present in Luke 23:35a. What we witness in Luke 23 is the intercalated use of τέρειν as *watch closely to effect destruction,* in this case, at the heel of the Crucified. Separately and together, the stories in Luke 7 and 23 also evoke the hope of Gen 3:15, drawing on the Hebrew, for a definitive bruising of the head of the serpent by the feet of the woman's seed. For Luke, that promise in Genesis comes to fruition in Jesus crucified and risen in Luke 23 and 24.

The book title Γένεσις is also inscribed throughout the words of Luke 7:44a, beginning at the first occurrence of γυναῖκα and ending at εἰς—

[44] γυναῖκα ... ἔφη· .... ταύτην ...εἰσῆλθόν ... εἰς

A close inspection of Romans 16:20a reveals that it has been incorporated into this section of Luke as well. Paul writes

---

2. Levine, "Pharisees in Luke," 122. Schiffman, "Pharisees," 619–22.

²⁰ ὁ δὲ θεὸς τῆς εἰρήνης συντρίψει τὸν Σατανᾶν ὑπὸ τοὺς πόδας ὑμῶν ἐν τάχει
And the God of peace will crush Satan under your feet swiftly.

Luke presents the principal terms in reverse order in his intercalations.

Σατανᾶς:

Οὗτος ἂν τίς καὶ γυνὴ ἅπτεται ἁμαρτωλός (Luke 7:39)

Συντρίψει/will crush:

ἕτερος..... αὐτῶν..... ἀμφοτέροις..... ἀγαπήσει (Luke 7:41,42)

εἰρήνης:

εἰρήνην (Luke 7:50)

Paul's rationale for his assurance regarding their crushing Satan under their feet is a moral one: "I want you to be σοφους / wise about the αγαθον /good, and innocent about κακον /the bad (Romans 16:19)".

These terms are distributed to the appropriate narrative receptacles:

Κακον/the bad—

ἐγίνωσκεν ἂν καὶ ποταπὴ γυνὴ
[in the thought of Simon] "he would know what sort of woman this is" (Luke 7:39)

Σοφους/wise—

⁴⁰ σοί φησίν. ⁴¹ χρεοφειλέται [depicts σοΦία /wisdom] (Luke 7:40, 41)

Αγαθον/good—

⁴⁴ ταύτην γυναῖκα; εἰσῆλθόν (Luke 7:44)

We note that in this rendering, it is the thought of Simon that is seriously defective, whereas the woman is acclaimed good, albeit subtly, through the mediation of Jesus Sophia.

Note as well Luke's stage directions in chapter seven that obliquely draw the reader's attention to the heel of Jesus. The Greek verb *stasa* can legitimately be translated *stand*. However, because she is in this moment also drying his feet with her hair, the verb also means that she simply *took her position* behind him; that is, near his *heel*. This choreography is well reflected in the rendering of the scene by the 19th c. French artist Jacques Tissot. This does not exhaust the potential borrowings of aspects of Romans in this Lukan text. The kiss of greeting among believers (Romans 16:16) is mentioned explicitly and "those things not able to be expressed in words" (Romans 8:26) is rendered in the woman's silence. In Romans 5, Jesus is presented as the new Adam who saves from sin and death. Uniquely among the canonical Gospels, Luke traces Jesus' lineage to Adam (Luke 3:38). In Luke 7 and 23, it is the feet of Jesus as the new Adam who saves from sin and death. What Paul outlines in schematic proclamation, Luke gives us as narrative elaboration.

Lest there be any doubt concerning the centrality of the foot-agenda here, we remember that it is introduced in Luke 7:34 by a saying about Jesus as glutton and drunkard. Similar phrasing is present in Deut 21:20 where it is followed by a regulation about those executed on a tree. As seen through this lens, Luke 7:36–50 indeed anticipates the cross of Jesus. Also from Deuteronomy is the woman's great love, a reflection of the Shema (Deut 6) that enjoins love for God. The name Simon [God hears] and the woman's demonstration of extravagant love derive their narrative coherence from Deuteronomy.

Insofar as the feet thematic is derived from Genesis the first book of Moses, and Simon and the woman derive their coherence from Deuteronomy, the fifth book of Moses, the Lukan narrator gives us a story exhibiting Pentateuchal unity. The Pauline parenesis in Romans 16:19, 20 provides Luke a more recent platform from which to shape his narrative. This Trifecta is only discerned when the reader recognizes the role played in the final production by intercalation.

The Intercalated Splendor of Luke's Conversation with Aratos

INTRODUCTION

THIS STUDY FOCUSES ON some of the ways in which Luke navigates between the twin horizons provided by a well-known Greek poet of the stars and the promise to Abraham that his descendants will be as numerous as the stars. It was born out of an experience of seeing afresh Greek letters that were there all the time, but the beholder wanting. I invite the reader to share that act of vision, knowing that for many it will initially seem as strange as it did for me, given our near-universal emphasis on fully formed words more than discrete vocables, integral concepts more than individual letters.

One needs also to remember as we begin that we are dealing with subtext, dependent for whatever weight it may carry on the explicit and primary text it subserves. It is a fact that the name Abraham occurs explicitly some fifteen times in the Gospel of Luke, more frequently than in any other canonical document of the New Testament literature. That underscores the propriety of exploring whatever subtexts involving this narrative character might be available to us in the Lukan *oeuvres*. And more than appropriate. While these background undertones remain subtext, not primary text, the task before us here is a new one and interesting. For example, the Abrahamic subtext with which the stellar theme is interwoven frequently supports the primary narrative assertion concerning the ability of Yhwh to communicate divine life against the odds.

In what follows, I treat several examples of sprinkled, or if you prefer, intercalated, dynamics. The word *intercalated* here means that Luke has chosen a particular vocabulary in his primary text that contains the correctly ordered individual letters of the subtext he also wants to convey. Thus the *modus operandi* that I propose in this space supplies one answer to the pointed question asked in Luke 10:26: "How do you read?" It is not a "higher" or "spiritual" reading. It resides firmly within the literal sense of the text as described in his own time by Cassian (5th c CE). Taking cues from Aratos, the reader discerns in a string of words a topic constituted by some of the letters in those Lukan words. The procedure is somewhat similar to a New Testament author's quote of a text from the Jewish Scriptures. The result in this case, however, is a subtext, wallpaper if you will, that is making a point about Abraham and Sara's progeny, frequently regarding some aspect of their numeracy.

One may reasonably expect that in a word search, the requisite letters will eventually turn up, if only one perseveres a sufficient distance. Of course, that is the case. Therefore, I have usually gravitated toward special Lukan material and favored those examples of Lukan editing in which the word sought presents itself in a comparatively brief compass as compared to its parallels elsewhere in the Synoptic Gospels. For example, the name of the constellation Σκορπιος is present in the similar sayings at Luke 12:39 and Matt 24:43–45. In Matthew, the requisite name is met at 42 words whereas in Luke we see it in only 8. This is a matter of art as much as science and I leave the reader to make those decisions on a case–by–case basis.

—The first order of business is establishing the probability that Luke knows and employs Aratos. Therefore, I offer an example of the influence of Aratus' *Phaenomena* on Acts 17 as well as Luke 1. These examples function primarily to illustrate that the Lukan author knows the work of this 3rd c BCE didactic poet as such who writes about the stars and the weather.

—Approximately a dozen allusions to constellations reside within the text of Acts, with attention to Abraham and Sara traditions as they appear in Genesis 11:27 –25:10.

—Approximately a dozen allusions to constellations are available within the Gospel of Luke, with attention to Abraham and Sara traditions as they appear in Genesis 11:27– 25:10.

The discussion of Luke's engagement with canonical Abrahamic traditions here should not be seen as diminishing the value of Abrahamic portrayals in the various recensions of the Testament of Abraham.[1] Yet that has already been explored at least to some extent by Lukan commentators. There is enough to do in the present venue with the canonical dialogue.

ΤΑ ΦΑΙΝΟΜΕΝΑ, ACTS 17, AND LUKE 1

The best recent critical edition by Douglas Kidd situates Aratos in Soli of Cilicia in the southeast corner of Asia Minor, active as a poet before 276 and probably deceased before 239 BCE.[2] Aratos' poem Τα Φαινομενα was well-known in antiquity, given ample commentary by Hipparchus, even rendered into Latin by Cicero and Germanicus, adapted by Vergil in the Georgics. Its 1154 hexameters depict constellations in the sky as signs given by Zeus to assist sailors in navigation as well as land-bound humanity in recognizing times for sowing. One feature of the poem asks the reader to attend to the visual layout of the letters λεπτη, slender/subtle. In Ph 783-84, the word occurs in a horizontal description of the new or crescent moon. In acrostic fashion, the letters λ—ε—π—τ—η also initiate each of lines 783-87. The purpose, in part, is to present a visual, vertical rendition of a slender moon. However, Luke is not bound to the acrostic pattern as such. In keeping with his leitmotif of Abraham's descendants as numerous as the stars, he

---

1. Sanders, "Testament of Abraham," 1.871–902.

2. Aratus, *Phaenomena* 3–5. [Here's Lukan at you, Kidd]. Volk, "*Letters in the Sky*," 209–40.

often scatters several letters that constitute a constellation of an idea in the Abrahamic tradition.

Acts 17

No one denies that Acts 17:28 quotes *Phaenomena* 5 του γαρ και γενος εσμεν [we are all offspring of (Zeus)]. However, this is preceded by the name of the poet Αρατος embedded in Acts 17:27

> Αρα ... αυτον ... ενος.

In Acts 17:29–30 appear the letters in the title of his poem Φαινομενα:

> Οφειλομεν ... αργυρω ... λιθω ... τεχνης ... ανθρωπου ... ομοιον ... μεν ... αγνοιας

Similarly, one finds in Acts 17:23 the letters of the names Σαρα and Αβρααμ scattered in the correct order:

> Διερχομενος γαρ και—
> Και ... σεβασματα ... ευρον ... και ... επεγεγραπτο ... υμιν

Genesis 15:5 is the pertinent referent here:

> He led him outside and said to him "Look up to the heavens and count the stars if you are able to count them. And he said to him 'Thus will be your seed."

This section of Acts 17 concerns Paul's speech in the Areopagus at Athens, on whose *altar (βωμον) to an unknown god* Paul is commenting. What follows in Acts 17:24 explicitly discusses *the God who made the heavens and earth and everything in it, this one being Lord of heaven and earth does not dwell in temples made by human hands*. The implicit subtext resides in Ph 408–10 in which the word for the constellation θυτηριον /Altar appears:

Yet even round that Altar ancient Night, sad for the suffering of men, has set an important sign of storm at sea.

The Intercalated Splendor of Luke's Conversation

The letters comprising θυτηριον/Altar are sprinkled throughout Acts 17:22a where Paul begins his speech. Note also that that the letters of the city name Αθηναι/Athens occur in Aratos Ph 408:

> Και... θυτηριον... αρχαιη. Luke has a potential resource here in Aratos for his choice of Athens as the site of his message concerning God's Just One in whom people may trust.

Aratus Ph 408–10 also says that the star Arktouros is opposite the constellation of the Altar. The diction of Acts 17:18 traces the contours of Αρκτουρος:

> Και Επικουριων και Στοικων αυτω σπερμολογος.

The final word σπερμολογος which gives us the last three letters of Αρκτουρος is a *hapax* in the NT. It is relatively rare elsewhere, though attested by the early 1st c CE rhetorical critic Dionysus of Halicarnassus when describing one Philonides as a *frivolous* fellow.[3] Dionysus also wrote a treatise on the arrangement of words and euphony, often given the English title of *On Literary Composition*. Perhaps we should look to this critic as one of the formative influences on Luke's constellations of letters. This thesis is all the more probable in that Acts 17:18 also contains an optative in speech, which had long since been neglected in spoken Greek but which Luke employs, perhaps as literary artifice.[4]

Luke rounds off this stellar excursion into Abrahamic territory with what has for centuries been treated in cursory fashion as a reference to an otherwise unknown female Damaris (Acts 17:34). In the textual world that we have entered, her name is in part a riff on the δαμαλις/heifer of Gen 15:9, constituting an initial offering of Abram to Yhwh. Moreover, this verse of Acts contains the sprinkled letters of αμμος/sand that constitute a terrestrial equivalent of the promise of numeracy like that of the stars.

> Και... ονοματι Δαμαρις... ετεροι... συν

---

3. Dionysus, "Excerpts: 19. 5, 1–4." See Cary, *Dionysus*, 346.
4. Moulton, *Grammar*, 197–98.

Gen 22:17 contains the divine promise to Abram that his seed will be not only as the stars of heaven but also as the sand at the lip of the sea.

If we were to secure a relationship between Aratos and Luke right at the beginning of the Gospel, we would be well on the way to a more leisurely treatment of a whole swath of residual data pointing in the same direction. To that task we now turn.

Luke 1

The eighth word in the opening of *Phaenomena* is αρρητον, unspoken:

> *Let us begin with Zeus whom we men never leave unspoken.*

The adjective is now widely seen as a sly pun on the name Aratos, the name of the poem's author. The eighth word in the Prologue of Luke 1 is πεπληροφορημενων, fulfilled. Its sixteen letters exactly double the poem's eighth ordinal position occupied by αρρητον. Furthermore, αρρητον itself is intercalated immediately after πεπληροφορημενων in Luke 1:1, 2—

> 1 πραγματων . . . 2 παρεδωσαν . . . αρχης . . . αυτοπται . . . γενομενοι

Note also that the opening of the *Phaenomena* (5–14) celebrates the celestial signs of Zeus as signaling the times of planting, of growth φοωνται, and harvesting of crops. Luke employs the word φοωνται in his editing of the Parable of the Sower, a parable also known to Mark and Matthew. Only in Luke 8:8 do we find this verb, twice, used to describe parabolic growth. In fact, Luke's use of the verb constitutes two of its three occurrences in the canonical New Testament.

What I find particularly compelling is that "unspoken," the adjective chosen by Aratos, coheres so well with the initial problem in the Lukan narrative. For his unbelief, Zechariah is rendered mute until such time as he communicates by writing the name of

The Intercalated Splendor of Luke's Conversation

the promised son to be born to him and Elizabeth in their old age. Such congruity complements the already striking set of data regarding the Luke/Aratos dialogue.

The interested reader will easily find in the remainder of Luke 1 the sprinkled letters of Λουκας (1:1), Αβρααμ (vs. 5), Σαρα (vs. 39), Ισαακ (vss. 37, 38), and αστερες/stars (vss. 55, 72–74). Luke's Zechariah and Elizabeth and the promised son of their old age John are a creative and reverent haggadic *homage* to Abram and Sara and Isaak.

——THE STARS/ ABRAHAM/ SARA SUBTEXT IN ACTS OF THE APOSTLES

Ara...tos occurs in Acts @ 8:22, 11:18, 12:18, 17:27, 21:38. These instances occur in conjunction with references to Παυλος or Πετρος, in whose names reside each of the letters in *Aratos*.

Constellations alluded to in the subtext of Acts include The Virgin and Crown, The Horse and Andromeda, The River and Altar, the Kneeler and Pleiades, Orion and the Archer, Skorpio and the Manger. In a category by itself at the end of Acts is the Deltoton, alluding to God as such. Note that the Manger begins the series in Luke and is penultimate in the series, occurring toward the end of Acts.

A word about the stellar framing of Acts is in order. Acts 1:11 adds to the cast of characters that it draws from Aratos. Ph 470–79 anticipates his readers' wonder at the circles of stars in the sky. Aratos imagines that

> someone else standing beside you has pointed out to you
> that star-emblazoned wheel (men call it the Milk).

After Jesus has ascended and the disciples' attention remains riveted on the sky, two men stood with them dressed in white garments. In their address Ανδρες Γαλιλαιοι resides γαλα, Milk. The last part of the frame in Acts of the Apostles involves the letters μελισσιου κηριον/honeycomb (Ph 1028–30) that also occur sprinkled in the last two verses of Acts, at 28:30, 31. This milk-and-honey frame complements that offered by the several Septuagintal samples of the phrase describing Canaan, such as at Lev 20:24. Together, these emphases engender the use of milk and honey in the parts of the Roman church known to Hippolytus [*Apostolic Tradition* 6] in the early 3rd c CE.

What follows are the points of contact between Acts of the Apostles and Aratos, in which we proceed through the points as they occur in Acts. Italicized words represent intercalations in the texts cited. Initial numbers represent chapters, followed by verse numbers; for example, 1 ... 14 represents Acts 1:14. For variety's sake and ease of reading I begin some sections with a citation of chapter and verse before naming the constellation whereas some sections I initiate with the name of a pertinent constellation before illustrating with chapter and verse.

1 ... 2–16. Some stars are bright and visible even when bathed in the light of the full moon, says A. at Ph 78–79. The words σεληνη/Moon (1:12), αστερες/stars (1:13), and εισωποι/visible (1:15) are sprinkled throughout Acts 1:12–16.

One may also detect the Παρθενος/Virgin constellation of Ph 97 in vs. 14 as well, where Mary, mother of Jesus, is mentioned. The Στεφανος/Crown constellation is discussed in Ph 71–73 where it is described as a memorial to Ariadne established by Dionysos. Each of those names is sprinkled throughout Acts 1:13–15.[5]

2 ... 1 αστερες/stars and Genesis 15:5.

3 ... 1 Ωριων.

This healing narrative in Acts sprinkles αστερες/stars throughout its first verse:

Ἰωαννης ... το ... ἱερον ... ἐπι ... της

culminating in an expression of the crowd's wonder and ecstasy in 3:10. The gate at which the healing transpires is Ὡραιαν, beautiful, attractive. One may be forgiven for wondering whether

---

5. One might wonder whether Botticelli's *Madonna of the Magnificat* had access to this tradition.

The Intercalated Splendor of Luke's Conversation

the constellation Ὠρίων also plays a role here. In fact, it is equally present in the diction of 3:1:

Ἰωάννης ... ἱερόν ... ἐπί ... ὥραν (Acts 3:1).

The constellation Ὠρίων appears in Aratos Ph 754 as part of the last circle of stars at the end of the solar year

ἔσχατον Ὠρίωνα

The word ἔσχατον is read by the ancient scholia as "the extremity/feet" of Orion. Kidd, however, reads the ἔσχατον adjectivally i.e. Orion bridges the last stellar circle of the year and the first.[6]

Let us suppose that Luke intends the ambiguous surfeit of both senses when he makes ἔσχατον part of Peter's address to the paralyzed man asking for alms:

Πέτρος ... χρυσίον ... ὑπάρχει ... τοῦτο ... ἐν (Acts 3:6).

Ἔσχατον mediates the sense of the New Age breaking into the old era. As allusion to the feet, it also serves as fitting background to the healing of someone paralyzed who is brought from sitting to standing, "walking and leaping and praising God", at the mention of the name of Jesus (Acts 3:9).

Echoes of Orion also occur in Peter's sermon Acts 3:11–26 explaining the significance of the healing that was reported in Acts 3:1–10. The sprinkled raw materials of his sermon seem to derive in part from Aratos Ph 587–88:

Ὠρίων/Orion has a ξίφος/sword and brings with him all the Ποταμός/ River constellation.

Ὠρίων: θεωρεῖτε ... εστερεωσεν (Acts 3:16)

Ξίφος: ἐπράξατε ... και. ... προφητων τον Χριστον (Acts 3:17,18)

Ποταμος: ἐπληρωσεν ουτως μετανοησατε υμιν οπως (Acts 3:18–20)

Peter's words cite the God of Abraam (Acts 3:13) who [via Paul in Romans 3:25] overlooks the ignorance of the past (as in the

---

6. Kidd, *Aratus*, 436—37.

case of God's treatment of Abraam). Peter's summons in Acts 3:19 to repent and turn for the removal of sin is also like that of John the Baptizer in Luke 3:1–20 where a river is implied, not stated.

3 . . . 6 The vocabulary here in Acts discusses silver and gold, holy and just. Though the gold and silver of Acts 3:6 may allude to their analogues in the Hesiodic eras, χαλκος/bronze is not explicitly mentioned. Bronze coins would be the type of small change given by many to those seeking alms at the Temple and we do see bronze that is sprinkled up front in 3:1, 2.

Προσευχης. . . ἐνατην. . . χωλος. . . κοιλιας

within a space of nine words. No χαλκος is on offer but healing in the name of Χριστος.

Another constellation plays a minor role in this narrative:

3 . . . 14. In Ph 96–139 Aratos describes The Parthenos constellation whose other name is Justice and the Ages of Man descending from gold, to silver, to bronze. He describes the descent into murder with a sword εινοδιην/ on the highway (highway robbery). In Acts 3:14, Luke uses the lament of Ph 132 to describe the choice of a bandit over Jesus at the Passion. He may also use it in the accusation of pilfering/embezzlement in Acts 5:3, 4.

5 . . . 1–11 Ananias/Saphira (The names begin with the same letters as A–braam/S–arra; possible meanings of the names Ananias and Saphira are borne out in the Abrahamic narrative of Genesis: *Yah has shown favor* Gen 14:19, *beautiful one* Gen 12:1 –13). The text in Acts here includes intercalated δεκατην/one-tenth (2x) and Μελχισεδεκ (2x): The conquest of enemies celebrated in Gen 14:20 may be represented in the denunciation of a Satanic presence in Acts 5. Tithing in Genesis 14 follows upon a battle involving loss of life. Acts 5 depicts two people losing their life following a dispute over contributions to the common good.

6 . . . 1, 7 contain the letters of Αβρααμ and αστερες/stars.

The Intercalated Splendor of Luke's Conversation

THE CROWN

Chapters 6-8 Stephanos/ the Crown. Stephanos, meaning 'crown', is both a personal name and the name of a constellation. Ph 572-76 discusses the constellation.

6 . . . 8 contains the letters of δυνει/setting. Aratos says that half of the setting/δυνει Crown is visible

8 . . . 3 while half is already cast down by the world's edge [Acts 8:3 contain the letters Στεφαν]

6 . . . 11, 12 These verses of Acts contain the letters of ὑπερτερα/upper parts and νυκτι/at night. Aratos says that the upper parts of the constellation Στεφανος move at night.

8:26-40 The encounter of Philip and the Ethiopian eunuch displays the following instances of letters reflecting the Abrahamic tradition of Genesis 22, the near-sacrifice of Isaac:

8:26 Αβρααμ; 27 Ισαακ are sprinkled throughout this verse.

32 προβατον/sheep is part of a *quote from Isaiah here*. However, κριος/ram is scattered in that same quote and reflects the ram of Genesis 22 who takes the place of Isaak.

40 χειλος/lip These letters occur as a distinct word in Gen 22:17 concerning the lip (shore) of the sea. The promise made in Genesis concerns the seed of Abraham who will be as numerous as the sand of the seashore. Acts 8:40 tips its hat to that promise by including the letters for lip in the portrait of Philip drawn to Azotus 4 km from the coast in the Shephelah region of the country. Acts 8:40, in a rhetorical flourish illustrating the innumerable sands of Gen 22:17, also explicitly says that *all the cities* of the region were given the good news by Philip. Little details like this justify the accolades given Luke as a stylist. But the presentation is even more extravagantly subtle. Philip travels northward along the coast to Caesarea. The region of *Ammon* [the word for *sand* as it occurs in Gen 22:17] lies to the east in the Transjordan plateau and parallels Philip's trajectory on the coast at least as far as Joppa, whose letters also appear sprinkled throughout the words in Acts 8:40. Gen 19:30-35, part of the Abraham narratives, posits the origins of the Ammonites in the youngest daughter of Lot. Her offspring solve

the problem arising from the narrative dilemma that Lot had no wife and the daughters no husband when they arrived in the area. Their initial infertility is typified in the Name Λωτ which letters are present in the Φιλιππος . . . Αζωτος of Acts 8:40. This subtext that takes account of Lot in Ammon may very well be the reason why Luke casts the Ethiopian traveler as a eunuch.

Acts 9 begins a fully developed portrait of Paul the apostle. Ph 427 supplies to Acts 9:3 the beginning of a frame that will find its completion in Acts 27. In this verse of the *Phaenomena*, Aratos discusses lightning (αστραψη) in the north with wind. Compare the explicit illumination (περιαστραπ-) occurring near Damascus, north of Jerusalem, in Acts 9:3 and the sprinkled letters of north wind (βορεω . . . ανεμοιο) in Acts 9: 8–10). Furthermore, Aratos assures sailors in danger at sea that Zeus is attentive to their prayers in such a circumstance and

> Despite their many travails, they will again look upon one another on board ship.

This Aratean text anticipates the assurance of Paul in Acts 27:34, 44 that not a hair of his shipmates' heads will be lost. Indeed, all came safely to land after the subsequent shipwreck.

THE HORSE

9 . . . 5 Ἑλικων Ph 205–24. The diction of Acts here conveys part of the story of the Horse constellation, whose hoof struck the earth of Mount Helicon, thus opening the

4, 5 Ἱππου κρηνην/fountain of the Horse Ph 221

18 Paul is baptized against the backdrop of mythological Hippocrene.

ANDROMEDA

9 . . . 39 Ανδρομεδα Ph 198
40 δεσμα/chains Ph 203
41 χειρες/hands (arms) Ph 204

The Intercalated Splendor of Luke's Conversation

Andromeda was daughter to an Ethiopian king (see Acts 8:27 and the Christological reflection on generation Acts 8:33b) and queen κασσιεπια/Cassiopia sprinkled throughout Acts 9: 36, 37. She was saved from her captivity at seaside [cp. Joppa on the coast Acts 9:36], by Perseus [intercalated in Acts 9:38], employing a Gorgon head [intercalated in Acts 9:39,40].[7] Peter is the apostolic focus in this section of Acts 9:36–43. His extension of his hand to raise Tabitha from death functions as antitype to the bound hands of the constellation Andromeda outstretched in Ph 203. Andromeda's release from her bonds by Perseus finds its analogue in the action of the angel breaking the chains from the hands of Peter in Acts 12:7. Furthermore, the reference to all of Andromeda's girdle (ζωματα) in Ph 201 finds expression in the instruction of the angel to Peter in prison "Don your belt (ζωσαν) . . ."

12 . . . 21 Ἡρῳδης/Herod and ἐρῳδιος/heron Ph 913.

22 επεφονει/shout and φωνη/voice. Aratos in Ph 914–15 describes the sounds of the heron whose erratic flight and loud cries indicate a strong wind stirring over the sea. A version of that wind appears in

13 . . . 2, 11, 26, 40, 41 when ανεμοιο is sprinkled into a statement about the Holy Spirit commissioning Barnabas and Saul at Antioch, a coastal city.

There is a temporary inability to see the sun explicitly presented in 13:11 and intercalated ἀστερες in 13:26. The "forgiveness of sin" (Acts 13:38) championed by Luke's Paul here operates under the umbrella of God's παρεσις, overlooking of previous ignorance, as in the case of Abraham (See Romans 3:25c). There is never a mention of Abraham's sin in Genesis 12–25. The letters of the word παρεσις are sprinkled throughout Acts 13:40, 41 (as also in Acts 17:30 where the explicit discussion concerns divinity overlooking of the times of ignorance).

---

7. Strabo places the provenance of the Andromeda legend in the city of Joppa on the coast of Palestine. *Geography* 16.2: 28–30. See Jones, *Strabo*, 274–75.

14 . . . 8, 12 Ορνις/bird is intercalated in Acts 14:8. In Acts 14:12, Barnabas is taken for Zeus and Paul acclaimed as Hermes during their work in Lystra. See Ph 269, 275 where a hazy bird constellation accompanies Zeus, and Hermes is remembered as carving a Lyra out of a tortoise shell.

15 . . . 7, 12, 13, 14. The νομηες (keepers of the sheepfold/shepherds) were the first to name Ἱππου κρηνη, says Aratos in Ph 220. Having presented an echo of Hippocrene in Acts 9, Luke turns in chapter 15 to an extended discussion of the relative importance of the νομος/Torah/Law among these early believers. The extensive stellar undercurrent of Acts accompanies a less thorough exploration of Law/Teaching when compared to Paul. Paul's stellar speculations, such as in 1 Cor 15, are minimal by comparison and his meditation on Law much more extensive (see Galatians and Romans).

16. . .16–28, esp. 27, αστερες

THE RIVER

16 . . . 12, 13 and the River Ph 358–61, especially 600.

Concerning vs. 12—The River was sometimes called the Ἠριδανος, intercalated in Acts 16:12 (within a space of 5 words).

Concerning vss. 13–14, Ποταμος/River occurs here as such (the only occurrence of the word in Acts). Ph 600 παρηοριαι "at its furthest extent" is intercalated here in Acts. For the Greeks, the River constellation's furthest reach is westward, then bends back toward the east, and the final section runs southwest. Cp. The itinerary of Paul in Acts 16:1—18:17—The call from the Macedonian district extending to the northwest of Greece, followed by his travel to Philippi and Thessalonica in the northeast of Greece, Beroea heading southwest, ending this Greek tour at Athens and Corinth in the south.

The Intercalated Splendor of Luke's Conversation

THE ALTAR [DISCUSSED AT THE OPENING OF THIS ESSAY]

18...1-6 "He spreads out the heavens like a tent for habitation" says Isa 40:22. As *tentmakers* offering hospitality to Paul, Aquila and Priscilla in Acts 18 are earthly complements to the focus in Acts 17 on the Altar constellation of the heavens. In the process, the transcendence of God as such is not forgotten. As in the first part of Is 40:22, the Sovereign enthroned above the circle of the earth [κυκλος/circle is sprinkled throughout Acts 18:1, 2] makes people seem as ακριδες/grasshopppers:

Μετα... Κορινθον... Ιουδαιον... γενει... προςφατως

A different reading of Acts 18:1, 2 attends to ουρανος/heaven as such:

Κορινθον εὐρων τινα Ιουδιαον ονοματι προςφατως

Αβρααμ/Abraam is then found in Acts 18:4-6.

Σαββατον διαμαρτυρομενος Ιουδαιοις ειναι αντιτασσομενων

Acts 18:1-6 functions between the twin foci of hospitality on earth and the stars of heaven, as in Genesis 15:1-5 and Gen 18:1-8.

THE KNEELER

20... 7-12 and Ph 617-21. Ph reports a star conglomerate setting and rising in the same night. The text attests to a commonly recognized designation for this starry character as the Kneeler. Eutychos is the sleepy character in Acts who falls from a third-floor window at midnight and is raised by Paul who continues to preach until dawn. Each of the letters in Ευτυχος are present in this excerpt from *The Phaenomena*. Aratos says that the full figure of the Kneeler awaits the appearance of Skorpio and the drawer of the Bow. The letters Σκορπιου are all present in Acts 20:11. Since Aratos names the constellation "the ever-kneeling", Luke also places

Jesus on his knees in Luke 22 in part to emphasize the symmetry in both "stars" setting and rising in quick succession.

PLEIADES

21 ... 7,8,9 Seven Πλειαδες, sisters, are intercalated here; Philip is cast as someone who had four daughters; and the address "brothers" is used in vs. 7.

Is this Philip one of the 12 (Acts 6:2) or one of the Seven (Acts 6:5)? One Philip or two? The number of the Pleiades is also disputed, 6 or 7 (Ara Ph 257–58).

ORION

Vs. 11 Orion, near the Pleiades, was known to Aristotle and Aratos as having a ζώνη/belt, which belt is explicitly named here. Zeus *assents* to/επενευσεν the Pleiades *signifying*/ σημαινειν the onset of plowing season (Ara Ph 267. In Acts 21:11, πνευμα reflects the letters of σημαινειν επενευσεν.)

Vs. 13 αροτοιο/ sow seed, plow is also intercalated here.

THE ARCHER

26 ... 12–18 Τοξευτης, The Archer (Ph 300–310) is intercalated in *Acts* 26:12. Ishmael is so described in Gen 21:20 and Ισμαηλ is intercalated in Acts 26: 12, 13.

14 Aratos Ph 306 notes that the Archer draws his bow near the κεντρον/stinger of Skorpios that rises at the end of the night Ph 304–5. To which Luke replies with

κεντρα (as a goad) in Acts 26:14.

The Intercalated Splendor of Luke's Conversation

SKORPIOS

See Σκορπιος intercalated in Acts 26: 14, 15 and the assertion that Paul's mission is to turn the people and nations from darkness to Light (Acts 26:18).

27 ... 1, 3. Aratos Ph 35-44 discusses the TWO BEARS constellations: The smaller and more faint of the two Κυνοσσουρα is the one by which Sidonians sail the straightest course. This constellation is embedded in 27:1 followed by the port-city of Sidon (27:3).

20 star-less dark at sea, sign of a storm ; So also in Aratus Ph 1013-18 [the theme occurs near the end of both texts];
20 χειμων/winter/storm
43, 44 *Perseus,* intercalated, effects a rescue at seaside

THE MANGER

28. ... 2, 3 sprinkles the letters of Φατνη, Manger [Cp. Ph 892, 898].
16, 17 cloudless under Φατνη/*Manger,* end of storm; Ph 995; flanked by two ονοι/asses
26,27 quoting Isa 6 that contains Αβρααμ, Σαρα.

DELTOTON

This Isaiah 6 quote is also congruent with the *isaiomenesin* triangle named *Deltoton in honor of Dios/Zeus* (Ph 235). Both of those terms in Aratos (i.e. *Deltoton* and *Dios*) are contained in this Isaiah 6 quote.

——THE ABRAHAM/ SARA/ STARS SUBTEXT IN LUKE

Aratos is intercalated @ 1:66; 8:25; 11:20, 21; 11:48; 12:42; 22:23. Each of these intercalated letters occurs in words quite close to one another, except at 11:20-22 where the discussion concerns *division* of spoils.

Constellations alluded to in the subtext of Luke include The Bear and Crab, The Manger, Lion and Asses, The Bull and Charioteer, The Eagle, The River and Dragon, the Bears and Wagons.

Again, italicized words represent intercalations in the texts cited:

This article began with attention to the Abraham Sara/ and Stars subtext in the earliest portion of Luke 1. However, now I turn to the influence of Aratos Ph 147-78 on the extended narratives concerning the conceptions and births of John the Baptizer and Jesus, as well as the early events in the life of Jesus (Luke 1 and 2).

In what follows, initial numbers represent chapters of Luke; For example, 1 . . . 36 = Luke 1:36

LUKE

and

THE BEAR

1...36,38, 39—41 Beneath the Bear's head are the Twins (Ph 147)

Head of the Bear κεφαλη αρκτου, beginning with και and ending with Μαρια, is sprinkled throughout these Lukan verses. While John and Jesus are not, technically, twins, there are many similarities between the presentations of the annunciations of their conceptions and births.[8]

2...3, 4 Aratos Ph 21-27 says that, as an infant, Zeus was deposited with two Bears who cared for him for a time. As a star-cluster they were also known as the Wagons. Should we not take this into account when both αρκτοι/Bears (Luke 2:3, 48) and Ἀμαξαι/Wagons` (Luke 2:4) are sprinkled throughout these verses about Joseph and Mary?

---

8. Brown, *The Birth of the Messiah*, See charts on 294-97.

THE INTERCALATED SPLENDOR OF LUKE'S CONVERSATION

THE MANGER

2...7, 15 Appreciating this point requires the reader to recall that the Manger is a cluster of stars at the heart of the constellation καρκινος, the Crab or Cancer.[9] The description of the child in the manger at Luke 2:7 contains within itself the letters καρκινος:
Ετεκεν αυτης πρωτοτοκον και εσπαργανωσεν αυτον αυτοις.-
I.e. The implied Crab καρκινος constellation contains the explicitly named Manger φατνη at Luke 2:7.

THE LION

Luke 2 . . . 8,9 Aratos Ph 148 says that under the Bear's hind legs the Lion constellation shines brightly.
The Lion/Λεων is present in Luke 2:8—
Φυλασσοντες αυτων. The splendor of the angelic visitor is made explicit in περιελαμψεν (Luke 2:9).

THE BULL AND CHARIOTEER

Luke's attention to these constellations bridges the scene of the birth of Jesus and his presentation and seminar with the doctors at the Temple in Jerusalem.
2 . . . 22 intercalates the constellation Ταυρος/The Bull
25, 26 Aratos Ph 167, 168 says that near the feet of the Charioteer constellation, look for the Horned Bull crouching.
See the letters of feet, ποδες, within the statement about Simeon in Luke 2:25
Προσδεχομενος.
And the Charioteer, Ἡνιοχου, is again embedded within this statement about the Holy Spirit's prediction concerning the Christ of the Lord at Luke 2:26
Κεχρηματισμενον ἁγιου Χριστον κυριου.[10]

9. Kidd, *Aratus*, 480.
10. Ἡνιοχ—concludes a brief amatory poem of the 6th c BCE poet

The Letters of the constellation Horned Bull κεραον Ταυρον are sprinkled throughout 2:29, 30 beginning with κατα and concluding with σωτηριον.

2 ... 34 Aratos Ph 177–78 says *But the Bull is always ahead of the Charioteer in sinking to the horizon, though it rises simultaneously*—Compare Luke 2:34 This [child] is set for the fall and rising of many.

ASSES

In Luke 2:20, still firmly within the birth scene proper, we find the letters ονοι/asses intercalated. Aratos Ph 898 identifies two ονοι/asses constellations on either side of Φατνη/The Manger. Might we assume that these constellations [the Bull and Asses] are the original influences on some of the animals placed in the creche of the Middle Ages and beyond?

By utilizing the lens supplied by this ancient poet of the stars, Luke's artistry celebrates the Abrahamic aspect of Jesus' birth, not only residing in the divine communication of life to an elderly couple as in the case of Zechariah and Elizabeth, but also to a young virgin, Mariam.

3 ... 23–38 and Gen 11:10–32 A genealogy precedes the extended presentation of the desert period of Jesus and Abram respectively.

4 ... 12 Of the three temptations presented to Luke's Jesus, in order of ascent, the third may be considered the most "stellar."

Αστηρ:

Αποκριθεις αυτω ειρηται εκπειρασεις

Anacreon. The poem addresses the παις παρθενιον βλεπων ... *lad who looks like a virgin* and acclaims him the charioteer of the poet's soul της εμης ψυχης ἠνιοχευεις. See Anacreon, 304 (4 B and D) in Page, *Lyrica*, 153. The name of the poet Ανακρεων appears intercalated in the frame of the narratives chronicling the child Jesus' early encounters with the Jerusalem establishment (Luke 2:22 and 2:52. See also παρθεν- in the description of Anna at Luke 2:36).

4 ... 20-23, 25, 26 In the inaugural sermon of Jesus in Nazareth, we find the letters of Αβρααμ (Gen 12 passim), Χαλδαι—*(Gen 11:31) [Babylon]*, a cited Ουρανος/heaven *(Gen 15:5)*, and intercalated Σαραι, this latter occurring in the one location Σαρεπτα Σιδωνιας (Gen 12:5).

7 ... There is a perceptible overlap between the narratives of Abram and his two sons and the intercalations in the account of the Lukan centurion and his servant/child.

1, Ισαακ; Ισμαηλ (Gen 21)
2, about to die (Gen 21:14 -16; 22:10).
3, ακροβυστια/uncircumcision (Gen 17:14), εστρατοπεδευσεν/ bivouac/move by stages in camps *(Gen 12:9)*.
3, 4 Αβρααμ, περιτομη/circumcision *(Gen 17:11)*.
7,8 διαθηκη/*covenant (Gen 17:10)*.
9, 10 faith/ δικαια/righteous (Gen 15:5).

There is also considerable overlap between the complaints about Jesus' diet and table companions and the stage props in the account of Abraham's encounter with Melchisedek:

33, bread and wine.
32-34 intercalated Μελχισεδεκ

8 ... 1, 2 In an account of Jesus' supporters among women, we find sprinkled ἐρημῳ/in the desert (Gen 12:9)
9 ... 9 In Herod's desire to see Jesus, we have intercalated Ισαακ...εν φυτω (Gen 22:13)
28, 29. The Transfiguration of Jesus reflects Aratos in Ph 476 as he discusses the radiance of the γαλα/Milk comprised of αστερες/stars.

Γαλα:

Εγενετο μετα λογους ἡμεραι

Αστερες:

Προσευξασθαι ... εγενετο ... εν ... προσευχεσθαι

10 . . . 17 A CHANGE OF WIND IN THE NORTH AND LIGHTNING (PH 427) IS ALSO PRESENT IN THIS SECTION OF LUKE.

βορεω δε παρ' ἀστραψη ανεμοιο. (Ph 427)—

βορεω:

Ἑβδομηκοντα κυριε εθεωρουν (Luke 10:17,18)
ἀστραπην (Luke 10:18)

ανεμοιο:

ουρανου πεσοντα δυναμιν του και ουδεν (Luke 10:18).

The Galilean Jesus' sojourn in and reflection on Samaria is congruent with this movement from north to south.

More significantly perhaps, Jesus speaks twice about heaven in Luke 10:17–20.

"I saw Satan falling like lightning from heaven" and "rejoice that your names are written in heaven." Satan the chief tester in the cosmic drama (as in *Job*) is giving way to the emissaries of God's reign in Jesus.

21 In a passage about the Sovereign of heaven and earth, intercalated αστερες/stars (Gen 15:5).

23 In a makarism about seeing, intercalated and interspliced *Aratος Φαινομενα*;

34, 35 In a parable about hospitality on the road, intercalated Αβρααμ

12:54 In a statement about reading weather signs, intercalated *Phainomena*

11 . . . 27, 28 The blessing on the womb that bore, the breasts that nursed, Jesus contains each of the letters of both Ισμαηλ and Ισαακ. Γαλα, The Milk in Jesus' response reflects in part the weaning of Isaak (Gen 21:8).

12 . . . 1–3 Both the poet and the title of his poem are present in these verses that sketch the appearance of things that once were hidden.

Αρατος:

The Intercalated Splendor of Luke's Conversation

Επισθναιχθεισων ... μυριαδων ... του ... ωστε

Φαινομενα:

Φαρισαιων ουδεν συγκεκαλυμμενον αποκαλυφθησεται

13-21 This text is special Lukan material. It begins with a request "Tell my brother to share the inheritance with me (vs. 13). Inheritance is the issue in Gen 21:10 where Sara moves to have Ismael excluded from any Abrahamic inheritance. The name Ισμαηλ appears sprinkled throughout Luke 12:13. This Ismael became an expert with the bow (Gen 21:20) which is important to Luke in that the constellation Τοξευτης, the Archer (Ph 300-302) is intercalated in Luke 12:15. Furthermore, Aratos conjoins discussion of the Archer with the rising of Σκορπιος at the end of the night. See the voice at Luke 12:20 "This very night your life will be required of you" and the intercalated presence of Σκορπιος at Luke 12:39 (again, within a space of eight words).

12 ... 49 I have come to cast fire on the earth (Gen 22:7 Father, here are the fire and the wood);

13 ... 10—17. Jesus enables a woman bent double to stand erect. Aratos Ph 570-74 says that the setting of the Ιχθυς/Fish constellation as far as the ῥαχις/spine coincides with the rising of the Crab in whose midst are the Manger and Asses.

Ιχθυς:

Ιδου εχουσα ασθενειας συγκυπτουσα (Luke 13:11)

ῥαχις:

προσεφωνησεν και χειρας (Luke 13: 12,13)

This is special L material.

15 Aratos Ph 892—98 says that the two όνοι /Asses constellation surrounds φατνη/The Manger constellation. Luke's Jesus discusses leading an ass in distress to drink. Watch the layout of the words: όνον ... ... φατνης ... ... ποτιζει. The ο ... ν ... ο ... ι surround the Φατνη. Hilarious Luke.

28 In a sentence citing Abraam, Isaac and Jacob at table in God's reign, we find the intercalated presence of αστερες/stars: εσται κλαυθμος των οψεσθε Αβρααμ εν βασιλεια.

16 ... 25-26 πατηρ πληθους εθνων (father of a multitude of nations) intercalated in the words of Abraham (Gen 17:4)

17 ... 11-19 concerns the healing of ten lepers and is special Lukan material. The pericope contains reverberations of Abrahamic tradition.

> For the sake of *ten*, I will not destroy it (Gen 18:32)
> With a *clean* heart, I have done this (Gen 20:5)
> Were not ten made clean? (Luke 17:17).

ARATOS IN PH 369-70 SAYS THAT FALLING UNDER THE FLANKS OF THE GREY HARE CONSTELLATION, THE STARS ARE ANONYMOUS

Του γλαυκου λαγωου ἐπεσεν ὑπο πλευρῃσι—
Luke 17:

11Τω πορευεσθαι Γαλιλαιας 12 αυτου κωμην λεπροι 13 αυτοι λεγοντες επιστατα 14 εγενετο τω αυτους 16 επεσεν τους ποδας 18 ὑποστρεψαντες αλλογενης ουτος 19 πορευου ἡ πιστις

The lepers here, like the stars, are νωνυμοι/anonymous.

17 ... 37

and

18 ... 13 Aratos Ph 507-23 states that when the earth is at its greatest distance from the sun the stars seen in that circle or zone display above the horizon three of their eight parts and the Eagle constellation is nearby; the Eagle, the messenger of Zeus (Ph 543). Three-eighths of the word count of Luke-Acts (word 14,166 of 37, 778) brings us to Luke 18:9 offering a warning against contempt for others via a figure who looks down upon a penitent praying at a distance in the temple, asking for the mercy of God.[11] A say-

---

11. The, 37,778 word count is offered in the commentary of Fitzmyer, *Luke I-IX* , 1.109. That brings us to the word εξουθενουντας Luke 18:9.

The Intercalated Splendor of Luke's Conversation

ing about lowering oneself and being raised up follows. Nearby in Luke 17:37 the eagles are gathered.

Appreciating a degree of symmetry between Aratos and Luke in this case might suggest that Luke-Acts in its entirety functions as a reminder of living in the waning light of the world's last era. Πυματον, a Homeric word that means "the last" is sprinkled throughout the gnomic word at Luke 17:37:

Ὁπου ... σωμα ... ἀετοι ἐπισυναχθησονται.Where the body is, the eagles also will be gathered. [The similar saying at Matt 24:28 does not permit this construal].

17 ... 28-32 Here, in what may be recognized through the lens of ἐσχατον as the final stage-set of the cosmic narrative, is a reminder of God's saving activity in Lot (Gen 18:20-21; chapter 19) saved from destruction.

... 34—37. These sayings concerning the end time reflect in part the text of *Phenomena* 313-315:

[There is another constellation] stormy (χαλεπος) when it rises from the sea (ἁλος) at the departure of night (νυκτος) and they call it the Eagle (αητος).

The word νυκτι is explicitly present in Luke 17:34, whereas αλος is sprinkled throughout αληθουσα in Luke 17:35. Αητοι, eagles, are explicitly present in Luke 17:37 and χαλεπος/ severe is sprinkled throughout Luke 18:1, 2 where we find the account of the judge and the pugilistic widow.

19 ... 5 Αναβλεψας/*having looked up* mirrors Gen 15:5 αναβλεψον to which is attached the promise about descendants as numerous as stars.[12]

9 Intercalated αστερες/stars precedes explicit mention of Abraam:

Αυτον Ιησους οτι σημερον εγενετο αυτος.

---

12. I see nothing objectionable in the recent suggestion that Jesus is the one short in stature in Luke 19:3. Soon "The Little Messiah" 151-70. If that is Luke's intention, Jesus would be following the stage directions of Genesis 15:5 and gazing up at one of the seed of Abraham.

THE DOG AND THE SCORCHER

19 . . . 2, 8. Aratos Ph 326–37 states that the Κυων/Dog Constellation *standing* on two legs contains the extremely bright Σειριος—
κυων:
Καλουμενος . . . .αρχιτελωνης (Luke 19:2)

Σταθεις taking a stand (Luke 19:8)

Σειριος:
Ζακχαιος ειπεν προς κυριον ἡμιισια (Luke 19:8)
All of this occurs under the soaring back of *Orion* (Ph 326).
Ωριων:

των ὑπαρχοντων κυριε πτωχοις τινος (Luke 19:8).

This again is special Lukan material.

19: 11–40 IN THIS PARABLE, A FIGURE LEAVES MONEY TO TRADE AS HE GOES AWAY TO BECOME KING. IN HIS RETURN WITH A BLESSING OF GOD MOST HIGH CONCERNING VANQUISHED ENEMIES, WE FIND SEVERAL INTERCALATIONS OSTENSIBLY ROOTED IN THE ENCOUNTER OF KING MELCHISEDEK AND ABRAM (GEN 14:17–20).

11 Αβρααμ
    15—16 Αβρααμ, δεκατην/tithe (Gen 14:20);
    17 ευλογ-/bless (Gen 14:19,20).
    23—26 Μελχισεδεκ (Gen 14:18).
    27, 28 Σοδομα (Gen 14:17)
    37—40 Μελχισεδεκ (Gen 14:18)

The characters who are praised in the parable are those who have increased their original bequest, thus enfleshing the logic of the promise to Abraham in Gen 22:17 "I will indeed bless you and multiplying multiply you".

THE INTERCALATED SPLENDOR OF LUKE'S CONVERSATION

20: 9—19. LUKE'S EDITING OF THE PARABLE OF THE EVIL TENANTS OF THE VINEYARD DISPLAYS A SPRINKLING OF THEMES FROM THE ABRAHAMIC TRADITIONS.

19 Ισμαηλ; *lay hands on (lay hands on* is unique to the Lukan account and appears in *Gen 16:12* as a description of Ismael*)*.

37, 38 αστερες/stars intercalated in Αβρααμ ... Ισαακ .. . εστιν ... νεκρων ... παντες

22 THE LUKAN SUPPER PRIOR TO THE CROSS AND RESURRECTION BEARS THE INTERCALATED SIGNS OF ABRAHAM'S ENCOUNTER WITH THE THREE VISITORS AND ITS IMMEDIATE AFTERMATH (GEN 18:1-19; CHAPTER 19).

24-30, 35-38 meal and judgment:

25, 26 Αβρααμ;

26 Ισαακ; nothing too difficult (Gen 18:13; see also Luke 1:37)

27 διακονων/serve at table (scattered in Gen 18:7)

28 Σαρρα intercalated here in Luke

Πειρασμοι/tests are explicit here and scattered among the letters of Gen 18:6.

Κρινοντες/*those who judge* are explicit here in Luke. Also see κρισις in Gen 18:19.

THE RIVER AND DRAGON

22...The Lukan Gethsemane scene has undercurrents of a dialogue with the constellations River and Orion as described by Aratos.

36 Αρατος; 36, 37 Ωριων/Orion; 37, 38 Ποταμον/River. Ph 588-89. Luke 3 has omitted the word River from the notices of Mark 1:5 and Matthew 3:6 that "many were baptized in the Jordan

River, confessing their sins". Luke 6:48, 49 presents the only explicit River in Luke and there it challenges the house without a foundation. Furthermore, the intercalated River that Orion and his sword brings up with him in Luke 22 may have been part of the inspiration for what has often been seen as a later textual insertion of vss. 43–44 concerning Jesus sweating drops of blood. I hear there an echo of the river turned to blood in Exodus 7:14–24, in part because the Lukan narrator uses the word *Exodos* to describe Jesus' Passion and Resurrection in Jerusalem (Luke 9:31). Therein resides the Jesus–centered River challenge to the house without a foundation.

That theme is complemented by the strengthening angel from heaven in these same verses (Luke 22:43–44) that may be read as reflecting Psalm 85 LXX. The conclusion of Psalm 85 LXX provides a potential template for understanding this scene.

> Give your strength (kratos) to your servant,
> And save the son of your handmaiden.
> Provide me a sign for good;
> Let those who hate me see and be ashamed,
> that you, Lord, help me and comfort me.

Luke's Jesus is God's servant, as his mother is female servant of God, apparent already in the first two chapters of Luke. And the strength sought by the Psalmist is embodied in the function attributed to the angel who "strengthens" (ἐνισχυων) Jesus. The Lukan angel fulfills the role of the sign for good.

Finally, "Father, forgive them, they don't know what they are doing" (Luke 23:34a has often been seen as a later insertion into the text but I would suggest that the text is not without a discernible rationale. It reflects the cluelessness of the Ninevites at the end of the Book of Jonah, thereby furnishing an example of a Prophet who complements the previous text from the Law (Exodos) and the Writings (Ps. 85 LXX). The risen Jesus in Luke 24:44 points out texts from "Moses, the Prophets and Psalms" that refer to him. These hypothetical insertions into the Lukan text may in part draw their initial inspiration from the River constellation of Aratos Ph 588–89.

The Intercalated Splendor of Luke's Conversation

The editorial insertions [Luke 22:43-44] are in dialogue with Aratos in yet another way besides attention to the River constellation. Aratos notes that in the world of the constellations, there is a location [on the horizon] where the end of settings (of constellations) and the start of risings (again, of constellations) *blend with each other* and that nearby is a toiling man on his knees (Ph 60 -70; especially 62, 65 -66). A uniquely Lukan assertion states that Jesus is on his knees (Luke 22:41), struggling in prayer. Δυσιες/ settings is soon intercalated in Luke 23:50, 51 concerning the burial of Jesus' corpse, even as αντολαι/ risings is intercalated in Luke 24:1 concerning the empty tomb. Joseph of Arimathea, in an interjected aside in Luke 23:51, is said not to have gotten *mixed up in* the decisions of the Council (hear the antithetical echo of Aratos' phrase *blend with each other*). What follows the text-critically stable Lukan assertion of Jesus on his knees in prayer (Luke 22: 42) is a passage text-critically suspect (Luke 22: 43-44), where we find an intercalated letters of δρακων/dragon. This reflects the δρακων discussed in Aratos (Ph 45-70). It, the δρακων, is near the point of swift settings and risings of constellations. Scribes inserted vss. 43, 44 containing intercalated δρακων partly so as to reflect the agenda of Aratos that heavily permeates Acts. These scribes thought it fitting to erect a dragon's edifice as Jesus enters in earnest into his Passion and Resurrection.

Yet another aspect of the Lukan Gethsemane scene is in dialogue with an Abrahamic text about the destruction of Sodom in Genesis 19.

Luke 22: 37, 38 include intercalated Σοδομα (see Gen 19:1); τελος/end is explicit here in Luke (τελος may be seen as intercalated in Gen 19: 28).

The scene at the cross of Jesus in Luke 23 transmits yet other intercalated Abrahamic traditions.

23....25 sprinkles within itself the letters of the name Ισμαηλ

Δια στασιν....βεβλήμενον....φυλακην...θεληματι

23...26 As Ismael was led away into a ἐρημω/ desert (Gen 21:14), Jesus is led away amid the sprinkled letters for desert:

Ἐπιλαβομενοι Κυρηναιον ἐρχομενον αὐτῳ

23...27 Hagar and her tears on his behalf (Gen 21:16) appear in sprinkled Ἁγαρ:

Λαου γυναικων ἐθρηνουν.

Jesus' words "Do not weep for me but for yourselves and for your children" are appropriate as a reflection on the Hagar narrative. So too his imagined projection of their future lament "Blessed the sterile and the womb that never bore, the breasts that never nursed." (Luke 23:29).

Jesus is also portrayed in the garb of Isaak, as early as the intercalation of Ισαακ in vs. 8, where Herod's desire to *see Jesus* reflects Abraham's seeing a ram for sacrifice at Gen 22:13.

Ισαακ occurs in the letters of Luke 23:28

Στραφεις ... ἀυτας ... κλαιετε

and again in Luke 23:30—

Τοις ἡμας και καλυψατε

Luke 23:31 mimics the focus of Isaak on wood at Gen 22:7 "Here is the fire and the wood"—

Jesus says "If they do this when the wood is green, what will they do when it is dry"? While the argument for Jesus as Ismael in Luke 22 is somewhat persuasive [desert/weeping], Jesus' genealogy in Luke 3 traces the line from Abraham to Isaac. Jesus is descended from Ishmael only in the sense that both are, in different senses, descendants of Adam.

47 κλαδος/branch; 49, 50 κλαδοι/branches [See the discussion of Gentiles grafted onto the olive tree of Abraham's faith in Romans 9–11, especially 11:17–24. The centurion in Luke 23:47 is a member of the εθνος/not exclusively Jewish peoples:

Εκατονταρχης ... θεον ... οντως

whereas the bystanders in 23:48, 49 are Ιουδαιοι/Judeans:

The Intercalated Splendor of Luke's Conversation

θεωριαν γενομενα τυπτοντες δε παντες οι γνωστοι.

51, 52 Αβρααμ

24. ...29 PERHAPS MOST STUNNING IN THE STELLAR UNDERCURRENT OF THIS CHAPTER BECAUSE IT IS HIDING IN PLAIN SIGHT IS THE REFERENCE TO ΕΣΠΕΡΑΝ/EVENING.

The name of the evening star Hesperos is legible in Hesperan... tou... syn. The letters of αστηρ/star are sprinkled throughout Luke 24: 29, 30. Well before Luke's time, there was a suspicion afoot that this star was the same as the one called Φωσφορος/Light-Bearer, Morningstar. Ovid Metamorphoses 11.296 says that it is that god who wakes the dawn and passes last from the sky. In Luke, the dual nature of the Morningstar and Evening star is approximated in the sudden recognition by "the two" that the stranger engaging them on their day-journey is (also) Jesus with them in their meal at night (Luke 24:31). While Aratos confesses (Ph 454-461) that he doesn't know what to say about such stars that change their positions, Luke has learned from other sources how to weave this story of Venus (aka Morningstar and Hesperos) into his articulation of the risen life of the Crucified on the move.

The resurrection editing in Luke 24 attends to an aspect of Abraham's reception of the three visitors in Gen 18:8.

42 The visitor eats a piece of baked fish——

Ἰχθυος ὀπτου μερος explicitly stated in Luke 24:42.

Should we have trouble envisioning the dish, perhaps we need look no further than this description of the meal Abraham set before the three visitors in Gen 18:6-8—

See sprinkled Μερος...ἰχθυος...ὀπτου—*piece of baked fish* within the following:

Σεμιδαλεως...ἐγκρυφιας...Βοας...καὶ...μοσχαριον..
.παρεθηκεν...αὐτοις...ἐφαγοσαν...παρειστηκει...ἀυτ οις...ὑπο

THE BEARS AND WAGONS

24. . . .51 Aratos Ph 21–27 says that the axis (ἀυταρ) of the revolving stars stays motionless and around it swirl the revolving stars. At either end of the axis are two poles (πολοι). On either side of the visible northern pole are two Bears (Ἀρκτοι) that wheel in unison and so are called The Wagons (Ἀμαξαι).

These terms are sprinkled throughout the conclusion of the Gospel of Luke and they initiate the Acts of the Apostles:

> Ἀυταρ:
>
> > Και ἐυλογειν ἀυτον ἀυτους ἀναφερετο"(Luke 24:51)
>
> Ἀρκτοι:
>
> > Ἀυτοι προσκυνησαντες ἀυτον ἐις (Luke 24:52)
>
> Πολοι:
>
> > Πρωτον λογον ἐποιησαμεν (Acts 1:1a)
>
> Ἀμαξαι:
>
> > Ἐποιησαμεν παντων ἠρξατο Ἰησους (Acts 1:1b)

CONCLUSION

Two remarks, concerning theology and a possible source of Luke's style, round out these observations.

Theology—

Allow me to suggest that the one yet unmentioned theological context significant for understanding Luke's attention to Genesis 11:27—25:10 is the hymn in Col 1:15–20—

> 15 He is the image of the invisible God, firstborn of all creation,
> 16 In him was created everything in heaven and on earth

visible and invisible, whether thrones, sovereignties, principalities or authorities.
17 He is before all and everything holds together in him.
18 He is the head of the body, the church. Who is the beginning,
Firstborn from the dead, that he might be preeminent in everything
Everything was made through and for him.
19 Because in him was pleased to dwell the whole Fulness,
20 Through him to reconcile everything to himself,
Making peace through the blood of his cross,
Whether things on the earth or in the heavens.

Luke employs this hymn's final verse (Col 1:20) in such a way as to lead to an allusion to Abraham in Luke 19:44. The verb ἀποκαταλλαξαι/reconcile in Col 1:20 is a *hapax* in the NT; indeed, I have not found another occurrence in Greek literature prior to this instance. The verb ἀποκαταλλασσ- is sprinkled throughout Luke 19:10, 11, beginning with ἀπολωλος in Luke 19:10 and ending with the sigma of *basileia* in Luke 19:10b. The parable of the reign of God that Jesus relates here ends with the murderous intent of its royal character to slay all his enemies, those resisting his kingship. A univocal identification of the king with God and/or Jesus hardly seems plausible. However, if we consider the occurrence of καταλλαγησεται in 2 Macc 7:33, we are on a more promising interpretative path. There, a mother and her seven sons are serially murdered by the despot. The unnamed mother affirms that whatever they may suffer for their sins, God will be *reconciled* to his servants, a reconciliation including their resurrection. That promised reconciliation of God with his servants, regardless of their success or failure in handling their gifts, is the primary sense of God's reign intended by the Lukan narrator. Reconciling all things ειτε τα επι της γης ειτε τα εν τοις ουρανοις/ whether things on the earth or things in the heavens is then sublated in the text of Jesus' entry into Jerusalem (from Luke 19:35b–37a), concluding with Jesus' lament that the city did not know the things that make for peace (Luke 19:42). A final lament that they did not recognize the time of their επισκοπη/ visitation (Luke 19:44) brings us to Genesis 50:24—

God will ἐπισκεψεται/ *visit* you and bring you... up to the land he swore to Abraham...

This Genesis verse is spoken to the Patriarchal line and anticipates the slavery in Egypt from which they will be freed. Hearing that liberative background in Luke 19 coheres with the description of Jesus' Paschal Mystery in Jerusalem as an exodos (9:31) and echoes the acclamation of the crowd at 7:16, "God has ἐσκεψατο/visited his people." Luke's fourteen total occurrences of εἰρηνη/peace are the most numerous of those in any of the other canonical documents in the New Testament literature. The accompanying Abrahamic themes, explicit and implicit, function in part to display a symmetry of events on earth and in the heavens being wrought by God in Jesus. This is not to promote the impossible wholesale perpetuation of first century historical realia, or deny the reality of ongoing, albeit somewhat intermittent, moral progress.[13] It is to assert the advent of the reign of God made apparent in the faith of Abraham and the person of Jesus and his church. Acts 3:21 insists that at present heaven must receive Jesus until the consummation of all things but he is assumed to be integral to that eventual consummation.

Furthermore, the Lukan author's attention to individual stars should not be allowed to obscure a more profound theological dynamic undergirding their particular identities, that of light. The primary referent of these lesser lights is the light of creation that Genesis 1 insists is created first, prior to sun, moon, and stars. The image in Genesis is that of a dome cut across with many sluices that, when opened in the night sky, allow light from above to shine through. That cosmogony is presupposed by Luke and elaborated in the frequency and placement of his references to light. There are ten such references to light. They begin in Acts 9:3 with the call of Saul to be apostle to the Gentiles and continue until the penultimate portion of the text at 26:23. These references to light

---

13. See Tanner, "Self-Critical Cultures," 223–56.

are bracketed by Isaianic quotes. Acts 8:32, 33 quotes the fourth Servant poem whereas Acts 28:26, 27 is a report of the negative response to Isaiah's message in Isaiah 6. I cannot believe that this attention to Isaiah is happenstance. The second of the Servant Poems says this "It is not enough that you be my servant, to raise up the tribes of Jacob and restore the preserved of Israel. I will give you as a light to the nations, that my salvation may reach to the ends of the earth." (Is 49:6). The trajectory of Luke-Acts is framed and filled with references to Abraham's descendants as numerous as the stars. Assisted by a studied engagement with Aratos, the evangelist celebrates their numeracy but also the splendor of their participation in the Light of Abraham's faith made visible in Jesus the Servant. The negative response on the part of some, duly recorded at the conclusion is, I think, a real but passing cloud (νεφελη intercalated at *Acts* 28: 24, 25), that Luke and his church hopes will give way to the splendor of the fully new creation. Until that Day, the author has left us a splendid witness to the divine communication of Life against all odds.

Potential Source of Luke's Intercalating Style—

Luke has carefully crafted a subtext to the Gospel and Acts of the Apostles concerning stars, Abraham, and Sara. That subtext provides the text with a considerable degree of literary unity from beginning to end. Recognizing it will, for most readers, be accompanied by a stunning realization that the component parts of the subtext, the requisite letters, have been there all along, right in front of our eyes. But whence does this intercalating procedure come?

I would suggest, though this is merely an educated guess, that we look to the earliest written Gospel for the answer to that question. The βασιλεια/ reign of God in Jesus, implicitly offered in Luke 24:37-39, reflects the implied presence of βασιλεια in Mark 7:32-35 and Mark 8:23-26. The Markan pericopae are traditions that neither Luke nor Matthew adopt. However, the material in Mark 8:29,30, 33 and Luke 24:39 adjoin presentations of the divine disclosure at the burning bush in Exodus 3:14 LXX where the issue turns on εγω ειμι ὁ ων. In their own ways, Mark and Luke are thinking through the contours of the reign of the I AM in Jesus.[14]

---

14. A learned critical note Edwards, *Quoting Aratus,* 266–79 denies Luke's direct use of Aratus. However, he did not consider the method employed in this study.

Letters, the Writing, and the Rock in John 7

³⁷ Ἐν δὲ τῇ ἐσχάτῃ ἡμέρᾳ τῇ μεγάλῃ τῆς ἑορτῆς εἱστήκει ὁ Ἰησοῦς, καὶ ἔκραξεν λέγων· Ἐάν τις διψᾷ ἐρχέσθω πρός με καὶ πινέτω. ³⁸ ὁ πιστεύων εἰς ἐμέ, καθὼς εἶπεν ἡ γραφή, ποταμοὶ ἐκ τῆς κοιλίας αὐτοῦ ῥεύσουσιν ὕδατος ζῶντος.
On the last day of the great feast, Jesus took a stand and cried out "If anyone thirsts, let him come to me and drink. The one believing in me, just as the writing said 'rivers of living water will flow from his belly.'"

STEP ONE: TRANSLATE TA γραμματα (John 7:15) literally as *letters*. Translating the phrase in 7:15 as *education* is unnecessarily paraphrastic. Far better to attend to individual letters as such when doing so expands the range of interpretative options for this chapter.

Step Two: When considering John 7:38, see Jesus the Rock following the people as in 1 Cor 10:4. The theme begins in Exodus 17 and Deuteronomy 8. After Philo takes it up and identifies the Rock with Sophia (*Allegorical* 2.86), Wisdom of Solomon 10:21—11:9 then furnishes to the Johannine author a toolbox of letters to portray Jesus as he does in John 7.

The letters of the book title Δευτερονομιον/Deuteronomy are interspersed in John 7:37–39 beginning at δε (vs.37) and ending at ῥεύσουσιν (vs. 38). Just as significantly, the letters of the phrase ἀκρότομος πέτρα/flinty, jagged rock (Deut 8:15) are interspersed in the invitation of Jesus in John 7:38 and are italicized here—

³⁷ καὶ ἔκραξεν... πρός... πινέτω. ³⁸ ὁ... ἐμέ,... ποταμοὶ ... κοιλίας... εἶπεν... τοῦ ·... γὰρ... ⁾πνεῦμα

The portrait of the flinty rock in Wis 11:4 is surrounded by discrete words such as διψ/thirst that also occur in John 7:37.

³⁷ Ἐν δὲ τῇ ἐσχάτῃ ἡμέρᾳ τῇ μεγάλῃ τῆς ἑορτῆς εἱστήκει ὁ Ἰησοῦς, καὶ ἔκραξεν λέγων· Ἐάν τις διψᾷ ἐρχέσθω πρός με καὶ πινέτω. ³⁸ ὁ πιστεύων εἰς ἐμέ, καθὼς εἶπεν ἡ γραφή, ποταμοὶ ἐκ τῆς κοιλίας αὐτοῦ ῥεύσουσιν ὕδατος ζῶντος.

In addition, Wis 10:21—11:9 includes sequences of separated letters that, when combined, form words reflecting the diction of John 7:38. In what follows, I cite words that occur in John 7:38 and then aspects of Wis 10:21—11:9. Compare

ἡ γράφη/the writing: Note the italicized letters ἡ γράφη in Wis 10:21—11:1—

ἡ... γλώσσας... ἔργα... προφήτου

ποταμου/river (see Wis 11:6)
κοιλιας/womb, belly: Note the italicized letters of κοιλιας in Wis 11:8, 9—

ἐκόλασας. 9 ἐπειράσθησαν ἐλέει παιδευόμενοι, ἔγνωσαν

ῥεύσουσιν/flow: Note the italicized letters ῥεύσουσιν in Wis 11:6—8—

6 λυθρώδει... 7 νηπιοκτόνου διατάγματος... αὐτοῖς... ὕ δωρ ἀνελπίστως, 8 δείξας... ὑπεναντίους

ὕδωρ/ water (Wis 11:4)

The thrust of John 7:38 suggests something very like that in John 4:14 "The water that I will give will become a fountain welling up to eternal life" but the specific diction of John 7:37, 38 is constructed with the building blocks just mentioned. Although the primary identification of the one experiencing the gushing water would be Jesus, that does not exclude the believers who are *in Christ* experiencing that water as well.

ASPECTS OF JOHN 7 BEYOND 7:37-38 AFFECTED BY THE PORTRAIT OF CHRIST AS ROCK

The phrase πέτρας ἀκροτόμου /flinty rock is also intercalated in John 7:7-10, beginning at περὶ (vs. 7) and ending with αὐτοῦ (vs. 10). The explicit Johannine narrative has Jesus following his brothers to the feast (John 7:10), similar to the Pauline assertion in 1 Cor 10:4 that the Rock *followed* the desert generation, and from that the people drank. Interestingly, πεπλήρωται/fulfill begins to evoke the sounds of πέτρα.[1]

Once one remembers the Pauline assertion that Christ is The Rock, even the concluding disputes in John 7 about the origins of *the Christ* when compared to the Law appear intelligible. The discussion of περιτομή/circumcision (John 7:22-24) that seems to have little to do with its surrounding context also bears a linguistic affinity τομ—with the adjective describing the Rock, i.e. ακροτομος/ flinty. This is a brief linguistic aside that remains centered in the chapter's chief image of Jesus. The single thread capable of bringing the reader satisfactorily from the beginning to the end of the chapter is that of Jesus as the Rock of the Torah's desert wandering period who follows and furnishes water to the thirsty.

---

1. Dodd, *Historical Tradition*, 322- 23, n. 4 asserts that in the opening of John 7 tracing the contours of Luke 13:31ff., John would have no motive for changing the Lukan τέλειοῦμαι. On the contrary, I would suggest that John chooses a verb of completion πεπλήρωται that echoes the sounds of his chief theme of Jesus as πέτρα/ The Rock.

The Beloved Disciple, Judas Iscariot

CENTRAL THESIS

WHY SHOULD ONE THINK that the Gospel of John alludes to Judas Iscariot as the Beloved Disciple? There are three major reasons:

1. In John 13:24, Peter asks BD to find out from Jesus the identity of the one who will betray him. BD asks Jesus and Jesus speaks to him but BD never gets back to Peter with the memo.

2. Also in John 13, once Judas has left the supper, we never again hear from BD at the Supper. Nor do we hear again about BD at the Supper.

3. The letters of the adjective ἀγάπητος/beloved appear in the correct sequence in two places in John 13 having to do with Judas Iscariot. The letters of the adjective ἀγάπητος are interspersed within the discrete words of these verses

    και γινομενου διαβολου παραδοι . . . .ἤδει τον παντες (John 13:2, 11)
    Ἰουδᾳ λεγει αυτῷ ποιεις ποιησον ταχιον ουδεις (John 13:26–28).

When the narrator in John 21:24 says of BD that he is the one who has written these things, the reader may reasonably think that BD is the same person described in John 13, Judas Iscariot.

Indeed, the letters of the name Ἰούδας are sprinkled throughout John 21:24:

²⁴ἐστιν ὁ ... μαρτυρῶν ... οἴδαμεν ... ἀληθὴς

This is the disciple who witnesses concerning these things and (the one) having written these things and we know that his testimony is true.

One may nonetheless also hold that John wrote this text. In the next article in this present collection, The Johannine Paraclete as an Index of Sorts, I point to evidence within the Farewell Discourse, John 13–17, that alludes to John as the author of the text.

For now, we explore first briefly and afterwards at length some of the tension between the portrait of BD on the one hand and the assertion that John is author of this text on the other.

SHORT ENDING TO THE BD JUDAS NARRATIVE

The decision that BD was John the Apostle has enjoyed a long tradition in the church. It proceeds from the claim of Irenaeus that he had heard Polycarp speak of John as the author of the Gospel. This claim is one that has generated the naming of persons and buildings, religious orders and foundations for over two millennia and there is little chance that this scholarship will change any of that in the future. I suspect that John was linked at an early stage to this text because he was, along with Peter and James, witness to the Transfiguration of Jesus in glory in the Synoptic Gospels and glory constitutes a recurring drumbeat within the drama of the Fourth Gospel. Be that as it may, the identification of BD with John is not part of the text itself. For those who are cautious about tampering with the truth of the gospel, it may be worthwhile to remember that this text does not mention the word gospel, either as noun or verb. The genre of the text is open for discussion. One may still hold that John shaped the narrative in such a way that its anonymous betrayer-turned-evangelist offers an identity with which some readers may want to identify. The phrase "Beloved

Disciple, Judas Iscariot" thereby becomes the approximate equivalent of "Good Samaritan."

LONGER ENDING TO THE BD JUDAS NARRATIVE

There are many things yet to say about the central thesis, not to enhance the proof but to elaborate for pleasure.

Again, there is something very odd about the events that follow Jesus' announcement that one of the disciples will betray him (13:21). I contend that only when we have let that oddity fully register are we in a position to identify the Beloved Disciple accurately. The text reads

> [21] After saying this Jesus was troubled in spirit, and declared, "Very truly, I tell you, one of you will betray me." [22] The disciples looked at one another, uncertain of whom he was speaking. [23] One of his disciples—the one whom Jesus loved—was reclining next to him; [24] Simon Peter therefore motioned to him to ask Jesus of whom he was speaking. [25] So while reclining next to Jesus, he asked him, "Lord, who is it?" [26] Jesus answered, "It is the one to whom I give this piece of bread when I have dipped it in the dish."[a] So when he had dipped the piece of bread, he gave it to Judas son of Simon Iscariot.[b] [27] After he received the piece of bread,[c] Satan entered into him. Jesus said to him, "Do quickly what you are going to do." [28] Now no one at the table knew why he said this to him. [29] Some thought that, because Judas had the common purse, Jesus was telling him, "Buy what we need for the festival"; or, that he should give something to the poor. [30] So, after receiving the piece of bread, he immediately went out. And it was night.

Odd is the fact that BD never gets back to Peter with the answer to Peter's question. Moreover, we never hear BD speak again at the Supper. The confluence of those facts suggests to this reader that the BD is none other than Judas Iscariot. As we watch Judas take the morsel and leave, we are watching the exit of the Beloved Disciple.

We now turn to some of the resources that may have helped engender and shape this portrait. Subsequently, we will think about the reception history of the BD question.

NARRRATIVE theology in dialogue with emerging Scriptures

The pleasures of Hellenistic literature
Nathan(ael) as preparation for the Judas theme
Nathan the prophet's parable (2 Samuel 12) and דוד
Judas, διαβολος and Satan
The Judas Iscariot Narrative as a Johannine Exorcism
Judas and Johannine Christology and Theology
Reconciliation of Judas
Swiftly (John 13 and 20)
Judas and Boat Crossing
Paradidōmi and parable
Jeremiah 50 and Romans 10 in the portrait of BD
Paradidōmi: Eucharist(ic) tradition and the intercalation of mercy
Judas/BD and the Spirit/Paraclete: A Different Kind of Latinism
Individual Disciples in John 21 called by two names
The Fourth Gospel of Judas/BD in the stream of disputed Pauline letters
The narrative time of the Fourth Gospel and the time of Judas' death
The hermeneutics of Judas/BD and the reign of God in John 21:1–14
Judas/BD and two agricultural reign of God sayings
Judas/BD and the mother of Jesus- individuals and paradigms
Narrating the mother of Jesus and Judas/ BD beginning in the Hour
    Investigating BD's trajectory in light of Song of Solomon 3:4 and the mother of Jesus

THE PLEASURES OF HELLENISTIC LITERATURE

Hellenistic literature was often understood to serve two functions. First, there was the function of διδασκαλια/teaching and associated utility. Secondly, there was the function of ψυχαγωγια/enthrallment and associated pleasure. The absence in John of the word ευαγγελιον/gospel and the absence of the usual word for prayer, προσευχ-, two basic religious categories of Christian antiquity, suggests to me that pleasure is a decided emphasis of the Johannine endeavor.[1] This seems especially so since enthrallment and associated pleasure were often understood to arise from the experience of hearing poetry and this text begins with an eighteen-verse excursion into poetic prose.

The text functions in part in service to the proclamation in John 1 that the only-begotten Son is on the Father's breast and is the Lamb of God. A variant of the combination occurs in the Beloved Disciple on the breast of Jesus. As evidence of the pleasurable gamesmanship that is present in the Fourth Gospel, I will be citing aspects of the portrait of Judas that follow on the heels of the rather different Synoptic portrayals. As noted, the lynchpin of the argument that Judas is BD resides in the early events of the supper in John 13. A few details in earlier chapters prepare for that event and its aftermath:

NATHAN(AEL) AS PREPARATION FOR THE JUDAS THEME

The narrative of John 1 puts the name Nathan on the Johannine horizon and serves as remote preparation in the upcoming narrative in John 13.

---

1. See Gutzwiller, "Literary Criticism," 340.

NATHAN THE PROPHET'S PARABLE (2 SAMUEL 12)

The parable told by Nathan to King David in 2 Sam 12:1–5 is key to the reading I am proposing here. It occurs after the arranged murder of Uriah and adultery with Uriah's wife.

> 12 The Lord sent Nathan to David. When he came to him, he said, "There were two men in a certain town, one rich and the other poor. ² The rich man had a very large number of sheep and cattle, ³ but the poor man had nothing except one little ewe lamb he had bought. He raised it, and it grew up with him and his children. It shared his food, drank from his cup and even slept in his arms. It was like a daughter to him.
>
> ⁴ "Now a traveler came to the rich man, but the rich man refrained from taking one of his own sheep or cattle to prepare a meal for the traveler who had come to him. Instead, he took the ewe lamb that belonged to the poor man and prepared it for the one who had come to him."
>
> ⁵ David burned with anger against the man and said to Nathan, "As surely as the Lord lives, the man who did this must die! ⁶ He must pay for that lamb four times over, because he did such a thing and had no pity."
>
> ⁷ Then Nathan said to David, "You are the man!
> [NIV]

The prophet, told to speak with David, tells a parable that depicts a rich man taking a poor man's beloved ewe so that he might slaughter it and feed it to a traveling guest. The analogue in John is the portrayal of Judas who steals from the common purse money intended for the poor (John 12:6). This is a uniquely Johannine comment. The other noteworthy aspect of the encounter with Nathan resides in the linguistic fact that the letters דוד can refer both to the name David as well as to the adjective "beloved." The analogue in the Gospel of John resides in the substance of this thesis, that the thieving traitor Judas, like David דָּוִד is also the beloved, **dōd** דּוֹד. There is precedent for such use of Hebrew elsewhere in the Fourth Gospel. As already noted, it is a surprising fact of the text that the word for Gospel/evangelize occurs nowhere in *John*. However, the Hebrew root ב-שׂ-ר offers a rationale for that omission, since בָּ-שַׂ-ר means "evangelize/bring good news" but in another vocalization, one of the other meanings of בָּ-שַׂ-ר is "flesh." The text of John goes to considerable lengths, in the prologue and in John 6, to insist that the Word has become flesh in Jesus. Given two alternatives for rendering a Hebrew word, the Evangelist emphasizes one much more than another. John 7:42 does mention David but the two occurrences there are not nearly as numerous as the frequent exploration of David's significance in the Synoptic Gospels. The parable of Nathan engenders the peculiar portrait of the beloved disciple in two distinct ways: by indicting him as one who steals from the poor and by insisting nevertheless on his status as beloved.[2] Judas, like the rich man of Nathan's parable, steals from the poor, and Judas is, like David, also the beloved. The Fourth Evangelist underscores his status as beloved by having him fed bread on the breast of the Master, similarly to the treatment received by the beloved ewe of Nathan's parable. With the exit of Judas from the Supper, we hear nothing more at the Supper from the Beloved Disciple, because, quite simply, they are one and the same narrative character. The Evangelist adds another indicator that we have here a dialogue with 2 Samuel 12. The ewe lamb is nurtured as a daughter among the poor man's children. Jesus in John 13:33 addresses the remaining disciples following the exit of Judas/BD as τεκνια/children.

JUDAS, DIABOLOS AND SATAN

In John 12 and 13, we have different chronological settings for the evil influence on Judas. Judas, identified as a διαβολος in John 6, fulfills that identity in chap. 12. Διαβαλλω means to bring charges falsely or with slanderous intent. Judas accuses Mary who anoints

---

2. According to the early 14th c. text *The Mirror of Man's Salvation*, the behavior of David serves as both a negative antithesis to and as an exemplary anticipation of aspects of the Gospel narratives. See the excerpt in Minnis, "Figuring the Letter," 159–60.

Jesus in the supper at Bethany. He charges her with waste of what might have been sold to assist the poor. Jesus challenges the charge by situating this moment of his presence within the yawning chasm of time in which the poor are *always* with you. John 13, however, situates the evil influence on Judas as betrayer within a different chronology. As the *Hour* of Jesus– lifted– up commences in a meal, Judas becomes Satanic. A similar dynamic is at work when the Lukan Jesus at that Last Supper refers to Satan's request to sift Simon like wheat.

THE JUDAS ISCARIOT NARRATIVE AS A JOHANNINE EXORCISM

Here I want to contest the notion that there is no exorcism in the Fourth Gospel. I suggest to the contrary that Mark 1:15, 21–28 provides ample reason to think that God's reign is exemplified in exorcism of a diabolic spirit. The Fourth Gospel lays the groundwork for its own version of that claim, beginning with the first appearance of Judas in John 6.

Full-fledged commentary has long noted that the phrase "the holy One of God" in John 6:69 echoes the cry of the possessed man in Mark 1:24.[3] The following verses suggest that part of the agenda of John 6 is to convey the advent of the reign of God as depicted in the first chapter of Mark:

> Mark 1:15 the reign of God has drawn near ηγγικεν
> John 6:19 Jesus drew near εγγυς the boat
>
> Mark 1:15 the reign βασιλεια of God
> John 6:15 they wanted to make him king βασιλεα
>
> Mark 1:15 repent/change your mind
> John 6:60 This word is difficult; who is able to hear it?
>
> Mark 1:15 believe in the gospel רָשָׁב
>
> John 6:47 the one who believes
> John 6:51 my flesh בָּשָׂר for the life of the world

---

3. Among the more thorough, see Keener, *The Gospel of John*, 1.697.

Mark 1:27 what is this?
Compare the question in Ex 16:15 mān-hû', *what is it*?
John 6:31 Our fathers ate manna
John 6:42 Is this not...?[4]

Mark 1:27 a new teaching
John 6: 45 they will all be taught by God
John 6:59 teaching in their synagogue

Mark 1:23 man with an unclean spirit
John 6:70 yet one of you is a devil

Mark 1:26 came out of him
John 6: 37 I will certainly not cast out

This Johannine variant of the Markan exorcism introduces the narrative of the end of diabolic influence on Judas. *Ergo*, there *is* an exorcism in John, that of Judas the Beloved Disciple.

JUDAS AND JOHANNINE CHRISTOLOGY AND THEOLOGY

The fact that the betrayer should be the one on the breast of Jesus makes sense in the larger context of this Gospel. As the Son on the breast of the Father in glory takes on the condition of humanity in its distanced condition of sin and death, so too beginning at the opposite end of the spectrum, the betrayer who actively embodies the mechanism by which sinful humanity will crucify Jesus is found on the breast of the enfleshed Logos.

The Judas thread is part of a tapestry whose main focus is the Son on the Father's breast. That divine reality became flesh in Jesus the Lamb of God. As that mystery makes its way in the world and especially as it appears among the first disciples called, the image suffers distortion within a sinful creation. However, the divine love supersedes distortion of the image by transforming Jesus' body in and for the world. It is perhaps no surprise that there is a tight

---

4. I think that it remains an open question whether the Fourth Evangelist is led to introduce discussion of the Son of Man by the Hebraic formula read left to right *hu-man*. This would have happened via the Latin *humanum*.

symmetry between the names Ιησους and Ιουδας. Of all the disciples counted as members of the Twelve, only the name Ιουδας is, like the name Ιησους, a two-syllable construction beginning with Iota and ending in Sigma. In the Johannine text, Ιουδας is the singularly appropriate literary exemplar of an aspect of who Jesus is and what he does in the world.

What is the theological rationale as such for depicting Judas as the Beloved? Quite simply, the Name יהוה bears within itself the shape of the letters דוד which means both "David" and "Beloved." Not only does Judas display the profile of the thieving traitor similarly to that of King David, so too the shape of the letters of their names and status as דוד resides within the shape of the letters יהוה. This is the same יהוה who loves the world, and who loves David and Judas in particular within the world.

Moreover, within the narrative theology of the Fourth Gospel, this question arises: if Judas functions similarly to David/BD, is Jesus then functioning similarly to Jonathan? Most decidedly, yes. The story of the friends David and Jonathan plays out within the scroll concerning the prophet Samuel. There are several parallels between Jonathan and Jesus:

> 1 Sam 18:4 Jonathan removed his garment
> John 13:4 Jesus removed his garment

> 1 Sam 18: Jonathan to David "my father does nothing either great or small without disclosing it to me."
> John 15:15 I call you friends because I have made known to you all that the Father has told me."

> 1 Sam 18:4 The voice of Jonathan——-"Whatever you say, I will do for you."
> John 14:13 The voice of Jesus——"whatever you ask in my name, I will do it." (Also see 15:7, 16; 16:23, 24).

> 1 Sam 20:39 only Jonathan and David knew the matter
> John 13 and 18: Jesus identifies the betrayer only to the betrayer

The very name Jonathan (the Lord gives) may be present in the formulation in John 4:10 *If you knew the gift of God . . .*

In his portrait of Judas, the Evangelist has utilized the image of David as beloved thief who is fed bread on the breast. Its complement, Jesus as friend-like-Jonathan is also present in this richly woven narrative tapestry of the Farewell Discourse.[5]

Though many ancillary details serve other functions, the equation between 2 Samuel 12 and the Fourth Gospel's BD is basically straightforward:
   David———-stole and had murdered———-a lamb, beloved as a child, on the breast of its owner
   Judas————a thief——-betrayed to death———-the Lamb of God, the Son, on the breast of the Father

Both David and Judas are treated as beloved by the Lord, a reading made possible in the alternative rendering of the consonants דוד as *beloved*.

RECONCILIATION OF JUDAS

I suggest that what we also see at the arrest of Jesus in John 18 is partly a development of reign of God material in Mark 1:21–28 that is relevant to the reconciliation of Judas. After his initial announcement of the advent of God's reign and his calling two pairs of brothers, Mark's Jesus exorcises a man who is convulsed and then freed from the influence of an unclean spirit. In John 18, the name of Jesus is explicitly interwoven with the self-description I AM, in the presence of a servant named Malchus, whose name sounds like the root מלך, reign/kingdom. Like the possessed man in Mark 1, Judas enters the scene under the influence, in his case, of Satan, and both scenes depict the effect of Jesus' speech on the bystanders. They are thrown to the ground. This scene limns the Tetragrammmaton and continues the soft drumbeat of Jesus as king that we have seen earlier in John 6.

---

5. Bede asserts that Jonathan's covenant with David prefigures the covenant of peace and love between Christ and the church. See Franke, *Joshua, Judges*, 276—77.

The Beloved Disciple, Judas Iscariot

Judas/BD, *ex hypothese*, repents at the arrest of Jesus in John 18. One might surmise that this happens when Jesus says "Let these (people) go." (John 18:8b). That language is redolent of the Exodus liberation and equally reflective of exorcisms in which Jesus says "leave person x." The implied beginning of repentance on the part of Judas in response to Jesus effecting the disciples' release seems confirmed in John 18:9 that reads, in a rather wooden rendering

> In order that the word that he had spoken might be confirmed:
> 'With respect to those you have given me, I lost from them no one'.

The attentive reader will remember that this is indeed what Jesus had said in the address to the Father in John 17:12. However, it is not all of what he said in that verse, which concludes with this qualifier: "except the Son of Destruction, in order that the scriptures might be fulfilled." The narrator in chapter 18 is now declaring that Jesus is making no exception to his claim that he has lost not one of the disciples. Judas as traitor is present as Jesus makes this claim. It is this moment, I would argue, that sets Judas as Beloved Disciple on a trajectory that will see him continue to follow Jesus.

There is a precedent for thinking that Judas changed his mind/repented, Matt 27:3. The outcome of that repentance ends tragically in Matthew with the suicide of Judas, but one may read the verb *metameleomai*, change of mind, in the Johannine verses concluding the arrest of Jesus in John 18:10–11—

> [10] μάχαιραν εἵλκυσεν αὐτὴν καὶ . . ὄνομα [11] εἶπεν Βάλε . . . τὸ . . . μοι . . . πατὴρ . . .πίω

Whether or not this is the case, in terms of classical dramaturgy the arrest of Jesus constitutes the *peripeteia*/turnaround of the Judas drama. From here, Judas as *the other disciple* and then *the beloved disciple* again follows Jesus to the courtyard of the high priest (18), to the cross (19) and empty tomb (20), and Jesus follows him to the other disciples in the upper room and fishing expedition (20, 21).

We would not be wrong to see the distinctive features of Jesus' behavior at the arrest as, in part, effecting a planned reconciliation with Judas. Jesus steps forward to identify himself in 18:4, 5 thus pre-empting any identification of Judas as the betrayer. This reconciliation with Judas/BD already began at the Supper insofar as Jesus indicates the identity of the betrayer only to the betrayer himself. No one else at the Supper knows what has passed between Jesus and Judas. Additionally, this Gospel has no Synoptic-like saying lamenting the fate of the betrayer. The Evangelist intends that the portrayed reconciliation between Jesus and Judas be complete.

Given the close association of Peter and Judas/BD in John 13, it would not be surprising to see that Judas is the other disciple who gives Peter access to the courtyard of the high priest (John 18). It is there that Peter will deny knowing Jesus, just as predicted by Jesus at the supper of chapter 13. Perhaps more significant for understanding the place of this narrative within the apostolic trajectory in the emerging canon at large is the fact that this uniquely Johannine stage direction in John 18 establishes a continuous line of witnesses to Jesus' words and deeds throughout the narrative to this point. Furthermore, if we take seriously the Judaic echoes in the threefold name of Judas, we can place Judas among the *Ioudaioi* who exchange words with Pilate. Judas' three names are reminiscent of some of the tribes of Israel:

Judah, involved in theft in *Joshua* 7:1, 16—18; cp. Judas as thief in John 12.

Simeon, in *Chronicles,* where he is always listed second; cp. Judas Simon in John 13:2.

Issachar, *Deut* 33:18, 19 claiming the abundance of the sea and hidden treasure in sand; and in 1 *Chron* 12:33 perspicuous in reading signs of the times; see BD in John 21.

These observations would not account for the personal exchange between Pilate and Jesus alone. However, the Judaic overtones of the name Ioudas approximate a narrative assertion akin to that in Acts 1:22 whereby the inner circle of disciples is privy to the Master's final words and deeds prior to his being taken up from us.

The Beloved Disciple, Judas Iscariot Swiftly (John 13 and 20)

Perhaps one of the more probative pieces of additional evidence in the thesis that the Beloved Disciple is Judas Iscariot resides in the adverb ταχιον. At the supper in chap.13, Jesus passes the morsel of bread to the traitor and says "What you are going to do, do quickly (*tachion*)" (13:27). In a direct echo of that movement, the disciple whom Jesus loves runs to the empty tomb more quickly (*tachion*) than does Peter (John 20:4). The diction is identical in these two instances. A near-approximation occurs in 11:29 when Mary arises quickly (*tachu*) to respond to the teacher's call. However, the key fits the lock exactly only in chaps. 13 and 20, opening the door further to the identification at the heart of this thesis.

Judas and Boat-Crossing

There is a discernible progression in the presentation of Judas in John chapters 6, 13, and 21. There is one boat (John 6:22), one betrayer (John 6:70). In John 13, there is the narrator's announcement of the passing over of Jesus to the Father (John 13:1) and his pouring water on his disciples' feet (John 13:4–20). John 21:3b–4a reflects aspects of each of those earlier events when we have the name of Ἰούδας incorporated into the verses describing the arrival of the disciples to the boat and their fishing expedition lasting throughout the night. Intercalation would suggest that *Ioudas* was at the boat when the others arrived. Begin at καὶ and end at Πρωΐας:

> καὶ ... τὸ ... νυκτὶ ... οὐδέν. Πρωΐας
> they went out and embarked into the boat and in that
> night they caught nothing. As morning...[6]

---

6. Another boat-crossing, in 2 Sam 19:19, three times employs the Hebrew root עבר in order to express that crossing. When used adverbially in the Hebrew Bible, it means "other." This may have influenced the portrait of Judas as the *other* disciple of John 18:15. Interestingly, with 2 Samuel 19, John 5 shares the themes of water, a lame man, return to Jerusalem, and lack of condemnation. Indeed, the numerical equivalent of the letters in עבר, based on their relative position in the alphabet, is 16, 2, and 20 which equals 38, the exact number of years said to be the length of time the man has been at the pool (John 5:5).

PARADIDŌMI AND PARABLE

John 21:20 claims that the BD is not only the source of tradition behind this text but is also the one who wrote it. That claim is partly rooted in the word *paradidōmi* /to *hand over*, that exhibits a negative sense of "betray" and a positive sense of "transmit." Given the claim of the data that BD is Judas, how true is the claim that Judas is the author? Here it is useful to attend to the parables that shape the story of Judas. Nathan's parable informs John 13, and the parable of the prodigal son shapes John 17–21. It seems to me best to view the claim about Judas as the beloved disciple and author in that parabolic light. Judas as author is true in the way that parables are true, teasing us by surprise into further thought.

JEREMIAH 50, ROMANS 10 AND THE PORTRAIT OF BD IN JOHN 21

As we progress through John 21, note that the words of Jesus in John 21:23 constitute a defense of Judas/BD:

"If I want him to remain until I come, what is that to you? You follow me"

and instantiate a thread of narrative theology in John that proceeds by utilising Jer 50:34 ("The Lord will surely plead their cause"). It is a part of a complex of themes in the Johannine Hour inspired by Jeremiah 50. The prophet's words in Jer 50:6 concern lost sheep who have forgotten/forsaken their fold. This theme anticipates Judas' action in leaving Jesus' breast in John 13. When Judas at the cross *returns to his own* he limns the sketch in Jer 50:16, 19. Furthermore, the fact that John 21:22 portrays Jesus defending Judas in twelve Greek words functions *sotto voce* to situate Judas/BD within the circle of the Twelve.

As for the influence of Romans 10, Judas/BD's belief at the empty tomb in John 20, insofar as it is resurrection belief, and his statement "It is the Lord' in John 21:7 together fulfill, precisely and completely, the Pauline prescription concerning salvation in Rom 10:9

> If you confess with your mouth that Jesus is Lord and believe in your heart that God has raised him from the dead, you will be saved.

At the very least, the portrait of the traitor as beloved is a somewhat more dramatic instance of the rehabilitation of a disciple such as the paradigm we have in Peter. It just so happens that this saving of BD also runs parallel to Paul's stated hope in Romans 9–11 concerning the salvation of Israel. In Romans, Paul reflects on the remnant of Israel whom he firmly hopes will be saved:

Isaiah cries out concerning Israel 'If the number of Israel's sons should be as the sand of the sea, a remnant shall be saved' (Rom 9:27).... thus all Israel will be saved (Rom 11:26).

One traitorous disciple saved in the Fourth Gospel bears some similarity to a hope in Romans 11 that all Israel will be saved. The nature of the similarity resides in the salvation envisioned, and not necessarily in the entirety of the background profile of the individual and the nation. The macro- portrait in Romans concerning the nation in its entirety may or may not be instantiated in the micro- portrait of BD. Perhaps we can fairly say only that the profile of Saul the persecutor who became Paul the Apostle may have exerted some influence on the portrait of Judas/BD in John 21.

PARADIDŌMI: EUCHARIST(IC) TRADITION AND THE INTERCALATION OF MERCY

The voice we hear in John 21:24 is similar to that of 1 Cor 11:23–26, evoked by reference to *betrayal, the supper,* and *the coming of the Lord*. In Paul, one writer speaks for the tradition held by many. *Paradosis* may mean both *betray* and *hand over*. In John 21:24, one author's witness and writing, what he hands over, receive common assent. However, whereas there is a formula of institution of the Eucharist in 1 Corinthians 11, the Fourth Gospel's author has scattered the elements of that formula throughout the Gospel in which there is no formula of institution.

Interesting in this regard is the influence of Wis 11:22–23 on the discussion of *paradosis* (John 21:20) in the sense of betrayal or sin, to which the divine response is mercy. The text in Wisdom reads

> 22 For the whole world before you is as a little grain in the balance; indeed, as a drop of the morning dew that falls down upon the earth.
> 23 But you have mercy upon all; for you can do all things, and overlook the sins of people that they should repent.

Ελεος/ mercy and δροσος/ dew are present in the italicized Greek letters of the verse below:

> And Peter turning sees the disciple whom Jesus loves following [them], who also reclined at the dinner on his breast and said "Lord, who is the one betraying you?"
> ²⁰ Πέτρος βλέπει τὸν ... Ἰησοῦς ... δείπνῳ ... Κύριε ... ὁ παραδιδούς ...
> ²¹ τοῦτον ... Πέτρος

Jesus effects the vision of Wisdom when he says "If I want him to remain until I come, what is that to you? You follow me." Other elements of Wis 11:22 present in the chapter include

- daybreak
- the seashore—grain (of sand)
- the whole world

Mercy shown this little world is an expression of the strength of the Lord's βραχιων/arm, the very image used to express the Lord's ruling power in Isa 40:10.

JUDAS/BD AND THE SPIRIT/PARACLETE: A DIFFERENT KIND OF LATINISM

Judas/BD is said to *remain* (21:22), as the Spirit remains on Jesus as witnessed by the Baptist in John 1. This is best seen as part of a Latinate exploration of VERITAS behind the Greek text.

Father—AUCTOR VITA

Son—ACTOR VERITAS

Spirit—VIA AUCTORITAS

The *remaining* of Judas/BD in the text occurs in the REST-that remains when VIA, the path of the Spirit/wind (see John 3) is abstracted from VERITAS. One may readily see the Father as author of VITA, life (as in John 5). The communication of that life through this text is the focus of 20:31. The witness of Judas/BD in this text is said to bear the marks of truth VERITAS in 21:24. Jesus the Son describes the Word of the Father that he embodies as VERITAS in 17:1. Judas/BD through this text functions as does the Spirit in bringing the hearers into communion with Father and Son.[7] Moreover, Judas/BD functions in at least two ways that reflect the linguistic meaning of the Spirit as PARAKLĒTOS, *one called alongside*. Judas/BD is depicted as being on Jesus' breast in John 13. Furthermore, he (along with the mother of Jesus) is the recipient of the blood and water flowing from Jesus' side at the cross to which he gives witness.

One can more fully comprehend the literary profile of the Spirit/ Paraclete in *the Fourth Gospel* by noting that Judas/BD functions as her human instrument through this text.

---

7. Kiley, "Latinity," 40–57.

INDIVIDUAL DISCIPLES IN JOHN 21 CALLED BY TWO NAMES

In John 21:2, two of the named disciples, Thomas and Peter, are also described by another name. I would assert the same for Judas/ BD.

THE FOURTH GOSPEL OF JUDAS/BD IN THE STREAM OF DISPUTED PAULINE LETTERS

The Fourth Gospel effects its parabolic witness of the one who both betrays Jesus and transmits his tradition in such a way as to evoke reminiscences of at least one letter written by a successor of Paul, that is, *Colossians*. We see the outline in John 21 of a claim made in Col 1:13 that believers are drawn from the realm of darkness into the kingdom of the Son of his love. In John 21, the fishing scene at daybreak includes the silent recognition that the disciples are indeed in the presence of the Lord (21:12) who then questions Simon Peter about love. The claim in Col 1:16 that all creation was made through Christ and for him is given partial expression in the miraculous catch of fish who are drawn to Jesus (21:11).

As he was present at the supper in John 13, Ioudas is also present in John 21:20–25, in a manner reflective of a theme in *Colossians*. As the narrator recounts BD on the breast of Jesus at the supper, he employs a form of the verb to *betray* that bears within it each of the letters in the name Ioudas, though in this instance not in the correct order. The word is *paradidous*, the participial form not used previously in the text but especially useful here as bearing within it the letters parADIdOUS/ IOUDAS. Secondly, as the narrative turns to reflection on the presence of BD in the written testimony of the text following his anticipated death, we hear about a report going out εις τους αδελφους, among the brothers, a phrase that also bears within itself the letters in IOUDAS: eIs tOUs ADelphouS. This dynamic seems to me a rather finessed instantiation of the theological truth expressed in Col 3:3

You have died, and your life is concealed with Christ in God.

At the close of both Colossians and John, the purported author of the respective documents is presented as situated within a circle of co-workers. In Colossians, the speaker points to co-workers in the plural—- *These are the only ones of the circumcision among my co-workers for the reign of God* (Col 4:11). In John, the co-workers as a group point to the author of the text—·—-*This is the disciple witnessing these things and who wrote these things, and we know that his witness is true* (John 21:24).

The fact that the Colossian text gestures toward the reign of God makes it even more likely that John 21, the codicil to the Johannine effort, adverts to a Pauline model whose theme is already, though subtly, integral to the Fourth Gospel. Lest there be any doubt that these conclusions to Colossians and John are in dialogue, note the intercalated presence of the phrase βασιλεια του θεου, reign of God, in John 21. The phrase βασιλεια του θεου is present in this section of John 21:20–23, highlighted here in italics:

²⁰ βλέπει ... μαθητὴν ... Ἰησοῦς ... καὶ ... λέγει ... ²² αὐτῷ ... τί πρὸς ... σύ ἀκολούθει. ²³ οὖν

[Note also the delightful double iteration of *the—-ou* in the phrase

ἀκολούθει.²³ ἐξῆλθεν οὖν [ʸ]οὗτος].

This is about as close as this author gets to clobbering us over the head with a stylistic distaff. That, and the fact that the name *Ioudas* is intercalated into John 21:24 and in the correct order:

²⁴ ἐστιν ὁ ... μαρτυρῶν ... οἴδαμεν .. ἀληθὴς
²⁴ This is the disciple who is testifying to these things and has written them, and we know that his testimony is true.

In sum, I suggest that John 21:24 consciously, though only partially, places the text under the aegis of pseudepigraphical activity already afoot in Pauline circles. The persona of BD in John as we have outlined it here is somewhat congruent with that of the traitor-turned-advocate whom we know in the Pauline corpus. Both betray, and both write. There is one further important distinguishing feature of the Johannine profile worth noting, however. No one steps forward in the text to say *I wrote this*. Therefore, we may be more accurate in saying that the more complete understanding of the authorship phenomenon is furnished by the *elite commons* championed in a recent title by Tom Geue. That author reports on various textual dynamics in antiquity that seem to suggest collaboration among literati who intentionally leave their collective deliberations unattached to any one author's name.[8]

THE NARRATIVE TIME OF THE FOURTH GOSPEL AND THE TIME OF JUDAS' DEATH

The saying in John 21:22 about the death of BD reflects a thread that began in John 12 and 13 where Psalm 41 supplied "the one who ate my bread lifted his heel against me." His mindfulness of the poor (though not actual care) in John 12 also reflects that Psalm's opening verse. Here, in John 21:22 is an echo of speculation about the death of the Psalmist "my enemies speak evil of me *when will he die and his name perish?*" (Ps 41:6).

However, can we say more?

Does the time of Judas' death negate the probity of this thesis that Judas is BD? Matt 27:5 is clear in its assertion that after Judas returned the blood-money *he withdrew and, going away, hanged himself*. The text is clear about the death post-dating the return of the blood-money but does not say exactly when or where the death occurred. Indeed, the ensuing purchase of a burial plot in Matt 27 is said to be *for foreigners*, and nothing further is said of Judas. Acts 1:18 is clear that Judas spilled his guts in more ways than one, his death known to the other apostles in Jerusalem after Jesus' Ascension to heaven. While these two witnesses differ as regards the manner of Judas' death, and do not state the precise time of his death, they may be seen as agreeing that he was dead

---

8. Geue, *Author Unknown*. The phrase *elite commons* occurs on 220.

by the time of Pentecost. If we presume that Acts was written prior to the Fourth Gospel or that its tradition about Judas' death was known to the Fourth Evangelist, does that not negate the thesis pursued here concerning Judas as BD in John? If one insists on the relevance of the historicity of the figure of Judas, and on his death prior to Pentecost, that leaves a space of some fifty days in which the events of John 20 and 21 may be situated. Indeed, the letters of the word for fifty, πεντήκοντα, are sprinkled throughout the last statement of the text. Begin at πολλὰ and end with τὰ.

²⁵ πολλὰ ... ἐποίησεν ... ἅτινα ... γράφηται καθ' ... οὐδ' αὐτὸν ... τὸν ... τὰ

I suggest that the Fourth Evangelist espied that opening and filled it with this vision of discipleship redeemed. As secondary support for this approach, note the heightened interest taken by the text in the issue of the time of Jesus' own death. After Judas is first introduced by name in John 6, the narrator repeatedly emphasizes that Jesus' own Hour had "not yet" come (7:30; 8:20). More importantly, the fact that the Fourth Evangelist never names the feast of Pentecost as such, despite his explicit interest in other feasts that he names, suggests to this reader that the vision he outlines concerning Judas has ongoing relevance in the church.

Is *Acts of the Apostles* important to this thesis concerning Judas as the Beloved Disciple? I would offer a confident "maybe." I like the way in which the trajectory of Judas as BD fits the chronology concerning Judas' death. It fits neatly within the parameters given by *Matthew* and *Acts*, providing a kind of pre-quel to *Acts*. As already stated, I think that the "other disciple" who gives Peter access to the courtyard of the high priest is the Beloved Disciple and modeled on the portrait of Paul in Acts 9, 22, and 26. In those chapters of *Acts*, Paul is repeatedly sketched as having received from the high priest(s) letters of authorization to persecute the church. However, even if the Fourth Evangelist did not know *Acts of the Apostles*, the portrait of a discipleship redeemed in Judas the Beloved disciple would still have its own integrity, based on tradition in the letters about Saul/Paul the persecuting beloved as well as the Davidic trajectory outlined above.

THE HERMENEUTICS OF JUDAS AND THE BASILEIA OF GOD IN JOHN 21:1–14

Luke 9:2 presents the Twelve as commissioned to preach the reign of God. John 21:1–14 intercalates the words *preach* and *reign* as well as aspects of the *BD* into its variation of Luke 9:2. In that process, Ioudas/BD plays an important role in our understanding of the 153 fish that depict Jesus' exercise of God's reign.

> 21 After this Jesus revealed himself again to the disciples by the Sea of Tibe′ri-as; and he revealed himself in this way. [2] Simon Peter, Thomas called the Twin, Nathan′a-el of Cana in Galilee, the sons of Zeb′edee, and two others of his disciples were together. [3] Simon Peter said to them, "I am going fishing." They said to him, "We will go with you." They went out and got into the boat; but that night they caught nothing.
>
> [4] Just as day was breaking, Jesus stood on the beach; yet the disciples did not know that it was Jesus. [5] Jesus said to them, "Children, have you any fish?" They answered him, "No." [6] He said to them, "Cast the net on the right side of the boat, and you will find some." So they cast it, and now they were not able to haul it in, for the quantity of fish. [7] That disciple whom Jesus loved said to Peter, "It is the Lord!" When Simon Peter heard that it was the Lord, he put on his clothes, for he was stripped for work, and sprang into the sea. [8] But the other disciples came in the boat, dragging the net full of fish, for they were not far from the land, but about a hundred yards off.
>
> [9] When they got out on land, they saw a charcoal fire there, with fish lying on it, and bread. [10] Jesus said to them, "Bring some of the fish that you have just caught." [11] So Simon Peter went aboard and hauled the net ashore, full of large fish, a hundred and fifty-three of them; and although there were so many, the net was not torn. [12] Jesus said to them, "Come and have breakfast." Now none

of the disciples dared ask him, "Who are you?" They knew it was the Lord. ¹³ Jesus came and took the bread and gave it to them, and so with the fish. ¹⁴ This was now the third time that Jesus was revealed to the disciples after he was raised from the dead.

Κηρυσσειν, preach, is present by intercalation, though never made explicit, in John 21:2, 3:

² Κανὰ τῆς . . . Πέτρος· Ὑπάγω . . . λέγουσιν . . ἡμεῖς . . . ἐξῆλθον καὶ ἐνέβησαν

What Jesus does here is an exercise in God's reign:

⁶ Βάλετε εἰς . . . δεξιὰ . . . πλοίου . . . εὑρήσετε. . . . καὶ . . . αὐτὸ

⁶ He said to them, "Cast the net on the right side of the boat, and you will find some." So they cast it, and now they were not able to haul it in, for the quantity of fish.

Ioudas/BD as such is not named as part of the original party who set out to fish. Yet he speaks in vs. 7. If he is an extra character added to the original party of seven, added without explanation as suggested above, the groundwork has been laid for an assertion about the new creation. How so?

Adding eight and the person of Jesus brings the count to nine. If we add and multiply the eight and nine, we will come to 153. That is, 8 + 9 = 17. Then 9 x 17 = 153. Listen to the language—-add and multiply——(increase and multiply). There are two identical commands given in Gen 1:22, 28—Increase and Multiply. That first creation is part and parcel of the new creation in Jesus.

This Johannine procedure seems to have traveled some distance from the description of the Twelve and their preaching the kingdom in Luke 9. The only number to the fore here is 153 and that, as we have just seen, appears capable of standing on its own two feet. However, this seeming distantiation from the Lukan witness is only partial. At the heart of both texts is a presentation of the reign of God in Jesus as received by the disciples. The difference between the texts may perhaps best be seen in relation to a figure who has played a subtle background role in John 1 and 20, that is, Hermes (John 1:38, 41, 42; 20:16). He gives his name to the process of translation and interpretation and, just as much to the point, he is, by some accounts, one of the Olympian Twelve.[9]

One of the twentieth century's premier Johannine commentators, Raymond Brown, sometimes plied an anecdote on the lecture circuit about somebody in heaven finally getting to ask the Evangelist how he arrived at the number 153 for the fish. The dry reply—"We counted them." The delight in that story is in no way diminished by an appreciation of the variety of ways in which hellenistic authors explored their respective languages.

JUDAS/BD AND TWO AGRICULTURAL REIGN OF GOD SAYINGS

The intercalated diction of chapter 21 accommodates at least two agricultural sayings about the reign of God:

—No one who puts his hand to the plow and looks back is suitable for the reign of God (Luke 9:62).

—Let [the wheat and weeds] grow together until the harvest (Matt 13:30). This saying is embedded in a parable whose interpretation ends with the promise that the just will shine like the sun in the reign of their Father (Matt 13:43)

Luke 9:62

Is there a benefit to be derived for our grasp of Judas/BD when we consider his story in light of the saying of Jesus about that plow? *Much, in every way*, as Plato might say.

> [62] εἶπεν δὲ ὁ Ἰησοῦς· Οὐδεὶς ἐπιβαλὼν τὴν χεῖρα ἐπ' ἄροτρον καὶ βλέπων εἰς τὰ ὀπίσω εὔθετός ἐστιν τῇ βασιλείᾳ τοῦ θεοῦ.

---

9. Seltman *The Twelve Olympians*. Hera, Zeus, Athenae, Hermes, Aphrodite, Hephaistos, Ares, Apollo, Artemis, Poseidon, Demeter, Dionysos. See 64—78 of Seltman for the messenger god.

The Beloved Disciple, Judas Iscariot

And Jesus said "no one who puts his hand to the plow and (then begins) looking back is suitable for the reign of God."

Stern words spoken by someone who himself has just embraced anew his destiny at the cross and beyond, and a saying unique to the Lukan portrait of Jesus. Just the kind of tradition that the Fourth Evangelist loves to preserve in transformed garb. There are three parts of the saying to be highlighted here:

a. No one who puts his hand to the ἄροτρον/plow
b. and then βλέπων εἰς τὰ ὀπίσω/looks back
c. is εὔθετός/suitable for the reign of God.

We pick up with the Johannine craftsman at John 21:15–22

¹⁵ Ὅτε οὖν ἠρίστησαν λέγει τῷ Σίμωνι Πέτρῳ ὁ Ἰησοῦς· Σίμων [a]Ἰωάννου, ἀγαπᾷς με πλέον τούτων; λέγει αὐτῷ· Ναί, κύριε, σὺ οἶδας ὅτι φιλῶ σε. λέγει αὐτῷ· Βόσκε τὰ ἀρνία μου. ¹⁶ λέγει αὐτῷ πάλιν δεύτερον· Σίμων [b]Ἰωάννου, ἀγαπᾷς με; λέγει αὐτῷ· Ναί, κύριε, σὺ οἶδας ὅτι φιλῶ σε. λέγει αὐτῷ· Ποίμαινε τὰ πρόβατά μου. ¹⁷ λέγει αὐτῷ τὸ τρίτον· Σίμων [c]Ἰωάννου, φιλεῖς με; ἐλυπήθη ὁ Πέτρος ὅτι εἶπεν αὐτῷ τὸ τρίτον· Φιλεῖς με; καὶ [d]εἶπεν αὐτῷ· Κύριε, [e]πάντα σὺ οἶδας, σὺ γινώσκεις ὅτι φιλῶ σε. λέγει αὐτῷ [f]ὁ Ἰησοῦς· Βόσκε τὰ [g]πρόβατά μου. ¹⁸ ἀμὴν ἀμὴν λέγω σοι, ὅτε ἦς νεώτερος, ἐζώννυες σεαυτὸν καὶ περιεπάτεις ὅπου ἤθελες· ὅταν δὲ γηράσῃς, ἐκτενεῖς τὰς χεῖράς σου, καὶ ἄλλος [h]σε ζώσει καὶ οἴσει ὅπου οὐ θέλεις. ¹⁹ τοῦτο δὲ εἶπεν σημαίνων ποίῳ θανάτῳ δοξάσει τὸν θεόν. καὶ τοῦτο εἰπὼν λέγει αὐτῷ· Ἀκολούθει μοι.

²⁰ [i]Ἐπιστραφεὶς ὁ Πέτρος βλέπει τὸν μαθητὴν ὃν ἠγάπα ὁ Ἰησοῦς ἀκολουθοῦντα, ὃς καὶ ἀνέπεσεν ἐν τῷ δείπνῳ ἐπὶ τὸ στῆθος αὐτοῦ καὶ εἶπεν· Κύριε, τίς ἐστιν ὁ παραδιδούς σε; ²¹ τοῦτον [j]οὖν ἰδὼν ὁ Πέτρος λέγει τῷ Ἰησοῦ· Κύριε, οὗτος δὲ τί; ²² λέγει αὐτῷ ὁ Ἰησοῦς· Ἐὰν αὐτὸν θέλω μένειν ἕως ἔρχομαι, τί πρὸς σέ; σύ [k]μοι ἀκολούθει.

And when they had finished their morning meal, Jesus said to Simon Peter "Simon, son of John, do you love me more than these?" He said "Yes Lord, you know that I love you" Jesus said to him "Feed my lambs." Jesus said to him a second time "Simon, son of John, do you love me?" He said to him "Yes Lord, you know that I love you." He said to him "Shepherd my sheep." He said to him a third time "Simon, son of John, do you love me?" Peter was grief-stricken that he said to him a third time "Do you love me?" And he said to him "Lord, you know everything, you know that I love you." Jesus said to him "Feed my sheep. Amen, amen I say to you, when you were young you girded yourself and went about where you pleased. But when you are old, you will stretch out your hands and another will gird you and take you where you do not wish." He said this signifying by what sort of death he would glorify God. And when he had said this he said "Follow me."

And Peter turning around sees the disciple whom Jesus loved following who also reclined at the meal on his breast and said "Lord, who is the one betraying you?" Therefore Peter seeing this one says to Jesus "And this one, what of him?" And Jesus said to him, if I want him to remain until I come, what is that to you. You follow me."

Note that the context of Luke 9:62 involves following Jesus, just as here. Note also the linguistic points concerning the letters of ἄροτρον /plow shared between the traditions:

Ναί, κύριε, σὺ οἶδας ὅτι φιλῶ σε. λέγει αὐτῷ· Βόσκε τὰ ἀρνία μου. ¹⁶ λέγει αὐτῷ πάλιν δεύτερον· Σίμων [b]Ἰωάννου, ἀγαπᾷς με; λέγει αὐτῷ· Ναί, κύριε, σὺ οἶδας ὅτι φιλῶ σε. λέγει αὐτῷ· Ποίμαινε τὰ πρόβατά μου. ¹⁷ λέγει αὐτῷ τὸ τρίτον· Σίμων [c]Ἰωάννου, φιλεῖς με; ἐλυπήθη ὁ Πέτρος ὅτι εἶπεν αὐτῷ τὸ τρίτον· Φιλεῖς με; καὶ [d]εἶπεν αὐτῷ· Κύριε, [e]πάντα σὺ οἶδας, σὺ γινώσκεις ὅτι φιλῶ σε. λέγει αὐτῷ [f] ὁ Ἰησοῦς· Βόσκε τὰ [g]πρόβατά μου. ¹⁸ ἀμὴν ἀμὴν λέγω σοι, ὅτε ἦς νεώτερος, ἐζώννυες σεαυτὸν καὶ περιεπάτεις ὅπου ἤθελες· ὅταν δὲ γηράσῃς, ἐκτενεῖς τὰς χεῖράς σου, καὶ ἄλλος [h]σε ζώσει καὶ οἴσει ὅπου οὐ θέλεις

The Beloved Disciple, Judas Iscariot

Simon loves Jesus and is being asked to express it in his care for [shepherding/feeding] the sheep of Jesus. In so doing, he will, as the intercalation insists, put his hand to the plow.

a. The stage directions then mirror those of the Lukan saying:

Ἐπιστραφεὶς ὁ Πέτρος βλέπει τὸν μαθητὴν ὃν ἠγάπα ὁ Ἰησοῦς ἀκολουθοῦντα.
And turning, Peter sees the disciple whom Jesus loves following.

The verb βλέπει matches exactly the diction of Luke 9:62. The italicized words επιστραφεὶς and ἀκολουθοῦντα function as a unit to express the idea of looking back.

b. Jesus' word in John 21:22 furnishes the text with an intercalated echo of εὔθετός, suitable.

Ἐὰν αὐτὸν θέλω μένειν ἕως ἔρχομαι, τί πρὸς σέ; σύ [k]μοι ἀκολούθει.

These three points of contact between Luke and John cohere best if we understand the text as presupposing that Simon Peter has come to understand that Judas is BD. After hearing about the difficult implications of his own love for Jesus, Peter gets curious about the future of one who had not simply denied in a moment of weakness, but methodically, and satanically, planned to betray Jesus. Yet Jesus will have none of Simon Peter's retrospective. For him, the proper focus in this instance concerning suitable behavior in the reign of God concerns the graced status of Judas/BD and his willed future until Jesus comes. Whether that status will be exercised in the flesh or through the witness of this text is left unstated.

Matt 13:30

The Evangelist in John 18:4, 5 prepares for the proper interpretation of the saying about weeds/ζιζάνια:

⁴ Then Jesus, knowing all that was to befall him, came forward and said to them, "Whom do you seek?" ⁵ They answered him, "Jesus of Nazareth." Jesus said to them, "I am he." Judas, who betrayed him, was standing with them.

⁴ Ἰησοῦς οὖν εἰδὼς πάντα τὰ ἐρχόμενα ἐπ' αὐτὸν] ἐξῆλθεν, καὶ λέγει αὐτοῖς· Τίνα ζητεῖτε; ⁵ ἀπεκρίθησαν αὐτῷ· Ἰησοῦν τὸν Ναζωραῖον. λέγει αὐτοῖς· Ἐγώ εἰμι. εἱστήκει δὲ καὶ Ἰούδας ὁ παραδιδοὺς αὐτὸν μετ' αὐτῶν.

The metaphorical identity of Judas as a weed immediately precedes the mention of Judas as traitor.

The letter of John 21:22 embodies the spirit of Matt 13:30. In Matthew we have 'Let the

weeds and wheat grow together until the harvest. In John, we have

If I want him to remain until I come, what is that to you? You follow me.

BD AND THE MOTHER OF JESUS- INDIVIDUALS AND PARADIGMS

The Evangelist handles the character of the mother of Jesus in much the same fashion as he does BD. While the Evangelist never names her Mary, and while he presents her as a recognizable individual, she also presents character traits that can be emulated by others. For example, her advice to *do whatever he tells you* in John 2 reflects Jesus' definition of anyone aspiring to be mother to him, namely someone doing God's will (Mark 3). In like fashion, the Beloved Disciple goes unnamed, never explicitly referred to as Judas. Yet he bears some of the lineaments of Israel as a people in the tradition and he provides the text's hearers with a paradigmatic example of someone growing in the life of graced discipleship to Jesus.

THE BELOVED DISCIPLE, JUDAS ISCARIOT

NARRATING THE MOTHER OF JESUS AND JUDAS/ BD BEGINNING IN THE HOUR

Thesean Propaideutic for Understanding the Mother of Jesus at the Cross of King Jesus

Theseus, first king of Athens, is represented in a long and variegated literary tradition. At a few points, his story displays affinities with the events of John 19.

—*tithēmi—lay down* is present in seven instances to describe Jesus laying down his life as event and model John 10: 15, 17, 18, 18; 13:37, 38; 15:13. The root in the subjunctive mood during the Johannine Hour contains many of the same letters as in the name Theseus. This usage has no parallel in the Synoptic Gospels.

—As king of Athens, Theseus accepts the children of Oedipus into his care as the old man dies. Somewhat similarly, the Beloved Disciple at the foot of the cross accepts the mother of Jesus as his mother.[10]

——Theseus is best known for his rescue of fourteen young people, male and female, from the labyrinth of the Minotaur to which they had been sent as human sacrifice. Symbolic representatives of the mothers and of the fourteen rescued by Theseus told stories in periodic festivals to commemorate the event.[11] Count the number of letters in John's characteristic way of describing Jesus' mother:

ἡ μήτηρ τοῦ Ἰησοῦ

Having seen who the Beloved Disciple is, it is time now to see the reign of God through the witness of John 20 and the text in its entirety. We consider—-

BD's "see and enter" actions and the reign of God
BD's trajectory in relation to Song 3:4 and the mother of Jesus

---

10. Sophocles *Oedipus at Colonus* lines 1630-40. See Lloyd-Jones, *Sophocles*, 580-83 and John 19:26, 27.
11. Plato *Phaedo* 58 A-C. See Fowler, *Plato*, 200-203.

CONNECTING BD'S "SEE AND ENTER" LANGUAGE TO THE REIGN OF GOD

It is difficult to find any commentary that clearly states the following fact: The language used about the reign of God in John 3:3, 5 ιδειν and εισελθειν, see and enter, also occurs in John 20:8:

> ⁸τότε οὖν εἰσῆλθεν καὶ ὁ ἄλλος μαθητὴς ὁ ἐλθὼν πρῶτος εἰς τὸ μνημεῖον, καὶ εἶδεν καὶ ἐπίστευσεν·
> Then the other disciple also entered, the one coming first to the tomb, and he saw and believed.

At this point in the text, we cannot be sure about exactly what he believed. But certainly, this language of this verse suggests at the very least that he is at the cusp of the reign of God. I suggest that we have watched the portrait of Judas /BD unfold since John 6, one in which he sees and enter God's reign according to God's will where he is intended to remain (21:22, 23).

INVESTIGATING BD'S TRAJECTORY IN LIGHT OF SONG OF SOLOMON 3:4 AND THE MOTHER OF JESUS

> *When I found him whom my soul loves, I held him and would not let him go, until I had brought him to my mother's house, to the room of the one who conceived me* (Song 3:4).

Let me proffer this verse as a structuring principle in John, a principle whose component parts we read beginning at the end of the text and moving backwards. The erotic language of the Song about two individuals serves the Evangelist as a vehicle for articulating the broader horizon of living in the many-membered Christ, beginning with Mary Magdalene and proceeding through to Judas/BD and the mother of Jesus. In a modified template of this Song, these narrative characters are both individuals and paradigms for believers at large.

WHEN I FOUND HIM WHOM MY SOUL LOVES

John 20:11—18
Mary Magdalene encountering Jesus risen intercalates the letters of *epithalamion/wedding song* in vss. 11, 12 as well as the letters of *agapetos*. The tone of their exchange outside the tomb evokes the chorus of boys and girls outside the wedding chamber, but with a difference. Whereas the youths and parents of the bride are urged to let go their hold on her to surrender her to the embrace of the groom (Catullus, poem 62) Jesus urges a release from embrace of him. That prepares for the attitude toward holding and letting go of others in various senses in John 20:23.

Catullus calls for the commitment of *foedus*/committed trust between lovers. Cp. Blessed those who have not seen, but believed (John 20:29)

> *I held him* εκρατησα αυτον:
> Those whom you hold, are held fast (John 20:23b)[12]
> ἄν τινων κρατῆτε κεκράτηνται
>
> *And would not let him go* ουκ αφησω αυτον:
> Those whose sins you forgive, are forgiven them
> ²³ ἄν τινων ἀφῆτε τὰς ἁμαρτίας [a]ἀφέωνται αὐτοῖς·. (John 20:23a)

Then begins the backward trek though John, focusing on the male beloved who has been given the mother of Jesus as his own. That relationship, to be shared by all believers, will proceed through a series of requests and the activity of God whereby the divine life in Christ is conceived.

UNTIL I HAD BROUGHT HIM TO MY MOTHER'S HOUSE

At the instigation of Jesus crucified in John 19, BD brings the mother of Jesus εις τα ιδια, to what is properly his own. Whether

---

12. This translation has been promoted in the new millennium by Schneiders, "The Resurrection" 186—87.

the content of εις τα ιδια is equivalent to the *house* of this verse of Song is possible but not a given. More likely and of more consequence is that the speaker of this verse of Song is no longer Mary Magdalene. Jesus is now the speaker of this verse of Song who is bringing BD (where BD = the one whom my soul loves) to where there occurs a repeated asking on the pattern of the Marian material in the early chapters of Luke. Here is how that pattern appears:

In John 14–16 the verb αιτειν is surrounded by the letters μητηρ mother in close proximity:

> ¹⁴¹³ καὶ ὅ τι ἂν αἰτήσητε ἐν τῷ ὀνόματί μου τοῦτο ποιήσω, ἵνα δοξασθῇ ὁ πατὴρ ἐν τῷ υἱῷ· ἐάν τι αἰτήσητέ [a]με ἐν τῷ ὀνόματί μου [b]ἐγὼ ποιήσω.
> And whatever you ask in my name I will do, in order that the Father may be glorified in the Son; whatever you ask in my name, I will do.

> **15** ⁷ ἐὰν μείνητε ἐν ἐμοὶ καὶ τὰ ῥήματά μου ἐν ὑμῖν μείνῃ, ὃ ἐὰν θέλητε [u]αἰτήσασθε καὶ γενήσεται ὑμῖν· ⁸ ἐν τούτῳ ἐδοξάσθη ὁ πατήρ μου ἵνα καρπὸν πολὺν φέρητε καὶ [v] γένησθε ἐμοὶ μαθηταί.
> If you remain in me and my words remain in you, whatever you want, ask and it will be done for you. In this is my Father glorified, that you bear much fruit and become my disciples.

> ¹⁶ οὐχ ὑμεῖς με ἐξελέξασθε, ἀλλ' ἐγὼ ἐξελεξάμην ὑμᾶς, καὶ ἔθηκα ὑμᾶς ἵνα ὑμεῖς ὑπάγητε καὶ καρπὸν φέρητε καὶ ὁ καρπὸς ὑμῶν μένῃ, ἵνα ὅ τι ἂν αἰτήσητε τὸν πατέρα ἐν τῷ ὀνόματί μου δῷ ὑμῖν.
> You did not choose me, I chose you and I have appointed you that you go and bear fruit and your fruit may remain, in order that whatever you ask the Father in my name, I will do for you.

> **16** ²³ καὶ ἐν ἐκείνῃ τῇ ἡμέρᾳ ἐμὲ οὐκ ἐρωτήσετε οὐδέν· ἀμὴν ἀμὴν λέγω ὑμῖν, [az]ἄν τι αἰτήσητε τὸν πατέρα [ba]δώσει ὑμῖν ἐν τῷ ὀνόματί μου.
> And in that hour, you will not ask me any questions. Amen, Amen I say to you, whatever you ask the Father he will give you in my name.

²⁶ ἐν ἐκείνῃ τῇ ἡμέρᾳ ἐν τῷ ὀνόματί μου αἰτήσεσθε, καὶ οὐ λέγω ὑμῖν ὅτι ἐγὼ ἐρωτήσω τὸν πατέρα περὶ ὑμῶν·
In that hour, ask in my name, and I do not say that I will ask the Father concerning you...

Note that the verb *aitein*, whether in the active or middle voice, occurs at nearly symmetrical intervals in these sentences:

Verse	Position of aitein; word number
14:13	5
15:7, 8	15
15:16	27
16:23	16
16:26	9

When these emplotments are sketched, they form a carat of sorts, pointing to the central command to *love one another* in 15:17. How is this love to proceed? *In his name*; but in what name? Ιησους of course. However, note that the openings of the first citation 14:13 and the fifth 16:26 are identical except for the position of the phrase ἐν τῷ ὀνόματί μου in my name, which has four words. I read this as a gesture toward the Tetragrammaton with which the name of Jesus is inextricably intertwined.

In addition, the context of the asking reflects the contexts, in correct order, of successive scenes in the Lukan conception and infancy narratives.

John 14-16	Theme	Luke 1, 2
14: 12-14	divine/human cooperation	1:34 -38
15: 5, 8	fruit	1:42
15: 15	made known	2: 15
16: 15-22	seeing at birth	2:30
16: 29-32	misunderstanding the words of Jesus	2: 50

All of the Lukan citations depict the conception, birth and growth of Jesus, and in all of them Mary plays a prominent role. Indeed, Jesus speaks in the analogous Johannine verses not only explicitly as Son of the Father but also implicitly as son of his mother. She is the door to what I think is one of the Fourth evangelist's most interesting programs because when we deal with Mary, we deal with the incarnation of the Word. The parallel tracks of the mother of Jesus and the Johannine disciples depicted in the table should come as no surprise to readers who hear Jesus say "if my word dwells in you . . ." The evangelist has carefully enfolded the requests of Jesus' friends in a presentation whose subtext points to the Lukan infancy narrative, suggesting that the proper and primary focus of all this Johannine converse is precisely the incarnation of the Word in the world. Or put it another way, the only requests that get answered affirmatively, but *all* of them, are those that extend in some way the incarnation of the Word in time and space.[13]

TO THE ROOM OF HER WHO CONCEIVED ME

Several motifs that follow the footwashing in John 13 evoke Marian dynamics of Luke:

Luke	John
The Almighty has done great things for me. . .(Luke 1:49)	Do you know what I have done for you? (John 13:12)
Behold the handmaid (δουλη) of the Lord (Luke 1:38)	No servant (δουλος) is greater than his master (John 13:16)
Henceforth all generations will call me blessed (Luke 1:48)	If you know these things, blessed are you if you do them (John 13:17)
Blessed the one believing that the things spoken to her by the Lord would come to completion (Luke 1:45)	I have told you this before it happens, so that you may believe when it does occur that I AM (John 13:19)

Finally, John 1:13 is the clearest reminder that the Jesus-event described here bears the contours of the mother of Jesus:

---

13. See Kiley "Johannine Discipleship," 87–92.

> Born not by bloods, nor from the will of the flesh, nor from
> the will of a man but generated by God.

The most direct narrative rationale for the association of Jesus' mother and BD is the word issued from the cross by Jesus (19:26, 27). However, there is also a Psalmic rationale for the association of the Mother of Jesus and BD. Psalm 8:6 extols Yhwh who crowns the Child of Humanity with glory. Ps. 103:4 does the same for Yhwh who crowns with faithful love.[14] The mother of Jesus is in a unique position to witness to the glory of God in the incarnation (John 1 and 2). She and BD are in a unique position to witness to the faithful love of Yhwh lifted up on behalf of Humanity (John 19-21). Together, they witness to the height and depth of the love of God in Christ as children of God are born from above/again.

Together, they witness a lance plunged into [ενυξεν] the side of Christ (John 19:34) after he hands over the Spirit. John 19:31-37 is unique to the Fourth Gospel. I read 19:34 as a response to the question asked by Paul in 1Cor 15:55b—

> ποῦ σου, θάνατε, τὸ νῖκος; ποῦ σου, θάνατε, τὸ κέντρον;
> Where o Death is your victory? Where o Death, is your sting?

The vision of the Evangelist is beautiful, profoundly so. It attests to the Evangelist's belief that the verification of Jesus' death at the same time points to the communication of the Spirit of Jesus who gives life without end. It takes up and instantiates the tradition reported by Paul in 1 Cor 15:3, 4—

> Christ died because of[15] our sins according to the Scriptures, was buried and raised from the dead according to the Scriptures.

---

14. A research report was presented by Joachim Eck at the 83rd (Virtual) International Meeting of the Catholic Biblical Association in Summer 2021. I was first led to think about these two Psalms in tandem with one another by the announcement of his report.

15. ὑπὲρ τῶν ἁμαρτιῶν ἡμῶν. This use of ὑπὲρ also occurs in Gal 1:4a. Many commentators choose to render this as "for our sins" with the meaning "for us in the situation created by our sins." So, for example, Fitzmyer, *1 Corinthians*, 546.

The work of the Johannine lance is part of a scenario envisioned by Paul that has Christ reigning [βασιλευειν] until all enemies are under his feet, the last of which is death (1Cor 15:25). Indeed, it is as king of the Jews that Jesus crucified speaks to his mother and BD words that remind the attentive reader of the will of God constituting them as his mother and sibling.

> Mark 3³⁵ ὃς [a]γὰρ ἂν ποιήσῃ τὸ *θέλημα τοῦ θεοῦ*, οὗτος ἀδελφός μου καὶ [b]ἀδελφὴ καὶ μήτηρ ἐστίν.
> Whoever does the *will of God* is my brother and sister and mother.

Look for the bolded and italicized letters of θέλημα τοῦ θεοῦ in the words of John 19:26–28a.

> John 19:26—28a ²⁶ Ἰησοῦς οὖν ἰδὼν τὴν μητέρα καὶ τὸν μαθητὴν παρεστῶτα ὃν ἠγάπα λέγει τῇ [a]μητρί· Γύναι, [b] ἴδε ὁ υἱός σου. ²⁷ εἶτα λέγει τῷ μαθητῇ· [c]"Ἴδε ἡ μήτηρ σου. καὶ ἀπ' ἐκείνης τῆς ὥρας ἔλαβεν ὁ μαθητὴς αὐτὴν εἰς τὰ ἴδια. ²⁸ Μετὰ τοῦτο
> Then Jesus seeing the mother and the disciple whom he loved standing there said to the mother "Woman, behold your son". Then he said to the disciple "Behold your mother" and from that hour the disciple took her to his own.

In short, the BD sees and enters the reign of God at the end of the text. His ongoing relationship with the mother of Jesus at the behest of the Crucified king, has him articulating a journey whose contours echo the voice of Jesus Sophia, whereby the One whose love has claimed him anew opens an avenue to the ongoing incarnation of the Word in the world. Such love is offered to all disciples (and the world), of course, but Judas/BD puts a distinctive individual face to that profile as a corrective to any use of the tradition that would make him an exception to the rule. His facilitation of others seeing and entering the reign of God stands under the horizon of Jesus' coming, however and whenever that occurs.[16]

---

16. The already/not yet dimension of the church's life in regard to the reign of God is still well-represented in Tillich, *Systematic Theology*, 3.300–423.

2. ISSUES OF RECEPTION AND THEOLOGY IN SUBSEQUENT TRADITION

Precedent of the Thesis
1 John 5:16, 17
Judas/BD and the Letter of Jude
The Names of the Twelve in the Book of Revelation
Irenaeus and his Ascription of the Gospel to John
The Creeds
Content and Its Expression
Judas/BD and Contemporary Relations between Jews and Christians

PRECEDENT OF THE THESIS

The thesis is not entirely new. In the late 1800s, a different set of arguments made the connection between Judas and the Beloved Disciple.[17] More recently, the massive study of James Charlesworth has included attention to the subsequent exposition of this theme.[18]

1 JOHN 5:16, 17

The profile of Judas as disciple-in-progress is present in schematic form as a paranetic model in the letter recognized by Raymond E. Brown and others as a commentary on the Gospel, that is, the first letter of John. 1 John 5:16, 17 says

> If anyone sees a brother commit sin that is not lethal, he will ask and God will give life to those sinning in a non-mortal fashion. There is such a thing as mortal sin; I do not say that you should ask concerning that. Every injustice is sin. And there is a sin that is not lethal.

The community's life is the zone of life, light, and love, leaving which zone plunges one into the realm of darkness and death.

---

17. Noack, *Aus der Jordanwege*. Griffin, *Judas Iscariot: The Author*. Overbeck, *Das Johanesevengelium*, 238.
18. Charlesworth, *The Beloved Disciple*, 170–79.

Such is the deadly sin. However, less grievous offenses that do not involve permanent excision from the community, as is the narrative case of Judas Iscariot, do not produce death.

The profile of Judas, furthermore, adds special poignancy to the thought of 1 John 4:10—It is not that we have loved God, but that God has loved us and sent his Son as a mercy-offering concerning our sins.

JUDAS/BD AND THE LETTER OF JUDE

One of the interesting byways revealed through this story of Judas the BD is the potential it bears for furnishing a better grasp of the letter that comes to us under the name of *Iouda*. The letter concerns God in Christ as savior, from beginning to end. Its verses 22 and 23 track aspects of the Judas/BD narrative in John 13 and 18 as we have described it. The exhortation there enjoins the hearers to save, with discrimination (as exercised by Jesus' demonstrated regard for Judas in John 13 and 18). Jude 23 also exhorts to save some as though snatching them from fire, an echo of John 18, Peter's apostasy that is facilitated by Judas *the other disciple*. The epistolary author in Jude 23 also exhorts to *save in trepidation* and adds *hating the very χιτών/ shirt stained by his flesh*. This makes sense as a vividly dramatic allusion to the garment stained by the beloved traitor who leaned on Jesus' breast (John 13).

What makes this profile in the letter so suggestive is the fact that the adjective "beloved", used only three times in the tract, traces in part the actions of Judas in the Gospel. Verse 3 mentions the faith handed over to the saints, expressed in the verb *paradidomi* used of Judas' betrayal in John 13:2. In verse 17, the author mentions words spoken by the apostles of our Lord Jesus Christ, a word concerning mockers who pursue their own desires. This is congruent with the disingenuous question asked by the thieving Judas/BD of Jesus "Who is it who will betray you?" (John 13:25). Finally, in Jude 20, 21, the author exhorts the hearers to be built up in your most holy faith, praying in the Spirit. Guard yourselves in the love of God. . . This gestures toward the scene at the cross of

THE BELOVED DISCIPLE, JUDAS ISCARIOT

Jesus when he hands over the Spirit after sending his mother to the domain of the beloved disciple (John 19:25–30).

In tabular form, these correlations appear thus:

Judas of the Fourth Gospel	—*beloved* diction in Jude
13:2	hand over vs. 3
13:25	mockers of the Lord Jesus vs. 18
19:25–30	build up one another vs. 20

THE NAMES OF THE TWELVE

One of the most interesting developments of the portrait of Judas/BD concerns his place within the enumerated Twelve who follow Jesus. John 6:70 places him squarely within the traditional list, while at the same time Jesus recognizes him as a devil. The variant of this verse in Luke 22:30 creates a particular problem that Luke and the Johannine tradition resolve in different ways. The Lukan Jesus at the Supper promises the Twelve that they will sit on twelve thrones judging the tribes of Israel. This would include Judas. *Acts of the Apostles* will replace Judas in short order after the Ascension of Jesus. However, that leaves dangling the question of the truth or efficacy of the promise made at the Lukan Supper to the Twelve, including Judas. Rev 21:14 portrays the heavenly Jerusalem in which the wall of the city is built on twelve foundation blocks and on them (are written) the names of the twelve apostles of the Lamb. Note, however, that the Johannine text does not provide the names themselves, only the number and their connection with the Lamb. Indeed, this assertion of the primacy of Twelve in the eschatological vision is etched by the Seer against a backdrop of the Word of God who bears a name that no one knows except himself (19:12). Such studied ambiguity in *Revelation*, naming the Twelve without naming them individually, leaves open the question of God's assessment of the grace or holiness of the Twelve and, most particularly in this current discussion, that of Judas. That judgment is and must remain God's secret.[19]

IRENAEUS AND HIS ASCRIPTION OF THE GOSPEL TO JOHN

I understand this notion of Judas the Beloved Disciple as entirely consonant with various emphases in church tradition except for those attempts in the second century to tie the Fourth Gospel to a figure named *John*. However, in those reports there is some ambiguity about the identity of the person under discussion. Irenaeus around 180 CE does identify the author as John, the Lord's disciple. I suspect that the Synoptic revelation of glory at the Transfiguration of Jesus to Peter, James and John may have been a factor in Irenaeus ascribing the Gospel to John, though he does not explicitly say so. The presence of *Simon/Peter* occurs only a handful of verses prior to the explicit revelation of glory in John 2:11, which might have been read by Irenaeus within that tradition of the Transfiguration.

Whether or not that is the case, Irenaeus certainly knew about a gnostic *Gospel of Judas*.

"They declare that Judas the traitor was thoroughly acquainted with these things, and that he alone, knowing the truth as no others did, accomplished the mystery of the betrayal; by him all things, both earthly and heavenly, were thus thrown into confusion. They produce a fictitious history of this kind, which they style the Gospel of Judas."[20]

This text to which Irenaeus refers, recovered and publicized in recent years, makes Judas the hero of a narrative that valorizes the divine spark in some humans and does not report any

---

19. Also attending to the Synoptic deposit and the veracity of Johannine witness is Beutler, *A Commentary*, xiii. *God's secret* is part of a larger discussion of office and sanctity in the church in Rahner "The Immaculate Conception," 1.204–5.

20. Irenaeus, *Against Heresies*, Book 1.31.1. In Roberts, *Ante-Nicene Fathers*, Vol. 1.358.

crucifixion of Jesus, perhaps implicitly disdaining such sacrifice.[21] One might well suppose that Irenaeus was happy to report his childhood memory of Polycarp's personal knowledge of John (*Against Heresies* 3.3.4) and assert that John authored the Fourth Gospel (though the latter is something never reported by Polycarp himself). In so doing, Irenaeus put some distance between the Fourth Gospel and a perceived gnostic threat to the faith. In the Fourth Gospel, as already noted, Jesus does not pronounce any woe against the betrayer. In The Gospel of Judas, Judas is the one disciple who understands Jesus' teaching about the special status of the elect. The fact that both the Fourth Gospel and the Gospel of Judas utter no Synoptic woe against Judas might have made the claim of the church Father seem even more urgent.

Nor was Irenaeus the only one laying claim to John as author of the Fourth Gospel. Ptolemy, a disciple of the gnostic teacher Valentinus, also attributed the Gospel to John. I judge Ptolemy's ascription of the Gospel to John to be one aspect of speculation centered on the name Ιωαννης. Its letters Alpha and Omega would be part of a meditation on the image of God in the Nag Hammadi Library (*Trimorphic Protennoia* and *The Egyptian Gospel*).[22] So the name John does indeed surface among the dueling camps of second century thinkers engaging the tradition. Within this context, Irenaeus staked a claim that was good for its time.[23] The thesis explored in this chapter, however, enables the church to understand the Johannine portrait of Judas within the horizon of emerging orthodoxy by seeing the parabolic and Pauline dimensions of the Fourth Gospel.

---

21. See the summary of scholarship by Burke, "Early Christian," 441–57, esp. 450–53. See also Brankaer, *The Gospel of Judas*. Pagels and King, *Reading Judas*.

22. See Layton *The Gnostic Scriptures*, 92, 107 n. 53d).

23. Heim, *Joseph Ratzinger* notes that Ratzinger has consistently emphasized the notion that revelation is more than Scripture and has at the same time championed historical investigation of the contexts of the Scriptural and dogmatic witness of the church. See especially his *Verbum Domini*.

THE CREEDS

The church is silent in her Creedal statements about the significance of Judas. The Nicene-Constantinopolitan Creed of the fourth century sets the boundaries, in schematic form, of the playing field concerning the church's understanding of God in Christ for the world. It does not mention Judas. The issue was not important enough to transmit in the Creeds.

CONTENT AND ITS EXPRESSION

I assume that in the Judas material of the Fourth Gospel, we are dealing with the same mix of history and theology that we have in each of the New Testament texts. We have long since recognized that there is some tension between and among many of the details in the canonical accounts of the Passion and Resurrection. This would be another to add to the list.

The thesis does not deny that a mystery of iniquity/sin was at work in the events leading Jesus to the Roman cross. It merely suggests another narrative means by which authors portrayed that iniquity.[24]

Thomas Aquinas, when thinking about truth's privilege in *de Veritate*, asserts that we should recognize truth as such, regardless of its source.[25] One practical ramification of this thesis is that we may be more forthright about the historical context of the art inspired by John's version of the Last Supper. The church may acknowledge that throughout most of art history artists and their patrons saw John as the Beloved figure on the breast of Jesus. That identification represents theology taking its cue from Irenaeus. That artistic instantiation is now complemented by another understanding of the dynamics of the Supper, no less apostolic at root, and furnishing its own nutritive value to the church's life of faith.

---

24. A principle championed at The Second Vatican Council by Pope St. John XXIII.

25. See also Burrell, "Analogy, Creation," 77–98 and O'Grady, "Philosophical Theology," 416–41.

For each of these reasons I have put forward arguments for consideration. They sensitize us to the relative presence of history and theology in each of the New Testament texts. These reflections also raise further ongoing issues: those things that the church considers central and what peripheral in her proclamation of the faith and the abiding significance of variety in the one witness of the written Word of God.

I recognize that others may interpret the data differently. Those not convinced by the arguments offered here may affirm in good conscience the danger that everyone sees in this story of Judas at the Supper: Mere participation in the common meal is of itself no automatic protection against infidelity to God in Christ. I join many others in saying so. I would simply expand that sensibility to include the probability that this text also envisions grace triumphing over sin in the lives of believers.

JUDAS/BD AND CONTEMPORARY RELATIONS BETWEEN JEWS AND CHRISTIANS

Astute readers will no doubt want to think further about the fact that the BD of the text bears some striking similarities to the profile of Paul as carried forward by his students/admirers/school. Since that bears so much potential to be used in sloppy or malicious ways against the adherents to Jewish faith and practice, it is well to remember that Paul expected that after a time of hardened resistance to the gospel among Jews, all Israel will be saved (Rom 11:26). The Johannine narrative of BD presents him as conveying a portrait of Jesus the Jew making claims from within Judaism about Jesus the Lord, claims resisted then as now by countless Jewish believers of good will. Until the day of days (Rom 11:8; Deut 29:4; Isa 29:10), we can expect that there will be vigorous debate, and (dis)agreement, about the meaning of the Jewish heritage then for relations between Jews and Christians now. An excellent articulation of that discussion is now available from the hands of Amy-Jill Levine and Marc Zvi Brettler.[26]

.... [Oh, was that Mark?]

---

[26]. *The Bible With and Without Jesus*

Postscript

DOES THE INTERCALATION DESCRIBED here have an afterlife; does this story have legs?
I offer the following final thought and invite the reader to decide for him or herself.

John 8:1–11 and the Reign of God
Few if any scholars now hold that the text of Jesus and the woman accused of adultery is part of the original text. However, it does bear the impress of dialogue with this saying in Luke:

> If it is by the finger of God that I cast out demons δαιμονια, then know that the reign βασιλεια of God has advanced εφθασεν among you.

Daimonia:

> Διδασκαλε . . . .κατειληπται . . . .μοιχευομενη . . . .ημιν . .
> . .ενετειλατο
> Teacher, this woman was caught in the very act of adultery and in the Law Moses commanded us. . . . . (vss. 4, 5)

[AND HE WROTE WITH HIS FINGER ON THE GROUND] (vs. 6)

Basileia:

Βαλετω ....κατακυψας ....εις ....κατελειφθη ....και
Let him throw the first stone...and having bent down he wrote on the ground...and he was left alone and (vss. 7—9)

Ephthasen:

Κατελειφθη ....και ....μεσω ....δε ....ειπεν

And he was left alone and the woman was in the middle. And Jesus said. (vss. 9, 10)

John 8:1–11, while crafted in the period different from the rest of the text, is nonetheless part of a recognizable trajectory reaching back to the earliest written canonical Gospel. The Johannine reign of God is not only writ large in the explicit statements of the text but also appears in the subtext that functions as commentary on it.

The Johannine Paraclete as an Index of Sorts

IN THESE OBSERVATIONS I argue that the portrait of the Paraclete in the Fourth Gospel has in view the sequence of the surrounding documents as we now know them. The Paraclete passages reflect distinctive themes of the surrounding texts Matthew, Mark, Luke, John, and Acts in that order. Discerning the integration of those Synoptic themes in the Paraclete passages will often be straightforward. In other cases, our grasp of what the author is doing is best achieved by attending to a dynamic that both antedates the Fourth Gospel by centuries and is also present around the year 100 CE, the date frequently suggested as the time of the text's composition. The focus of the thesis is a limited one, but I suggest that it marks a genuine step forward in our understanding of what the composer hoped to achieve by attending to what s/he describes as the Paraclete.

THESIS

Firstly, the passages we consider are
John 14:16; 14:26; 15:26; 16:8–11 and 16:12–15.

14:16 κἀγὼ ἐρωτήσω τὸν πατέρα καὶ ἄλλον παράκλητον δώσει ὑμῖν ἵνα ᾖ μεθ' ὑμῶν εἰς τὸν] αἰῶνα

And I will ask the Father and he will give you another Paraclete to be with you forever.

14:26 ὁ δὲ παράκλητος, τὸ πνεῦμα τὸ ἅγιον ὃ πέμψει ὁ πατὴρ ἐν τῷ ὀνόματί μου, ἐκεῖνος ὑμᾶς διδάξει πάντα καὶ ὑπομνήσει ὑμᾶς πάντα ἃ εἶπον [af]ὑμῖν.

And the Paraclete, the Holy Spirit, whom the Father will send in my Name, that one will teach you everything and remind you of everything I have told you.

15:26 Ὅταν ἔλθῃ ὁ παράκλητος ὃν ἐγὼ πέμψω ὑμῖν παρὰ τοῦ πατρός, τὸ πνεῦμα τῆς ἀληθείας ὃ παρὰ τοῦ πατρὸς ἐκπορεύεται, ἐκεῖνος μαρτυρήσει περὶ ἐμοῦ·

When the Paraclete comes whom I will send you from the Father, the Spirit of Truth who proceeds from the Father, that one will witness concerning me.

16:7–15

⁷ ἀλλ' ἐγὼ τὴν ἀλήθειαν λέγω ὑμῖν, συμφέρει ὑμῖν ἵνα ἐγὼ ἀπέλθω. ἐὰν [c]γὰρ μὴ ἀπέλθω, ὁ παράκλητος [d]οὐ μὴ ἔλθῃ πρὸς ὑμᾶς· ἐὰν δὲ πορευθῶ, πέμψω αὐτὸν πρὸς ὑμᾶς. ⁸ καὶ ἐλθὼν ἐκεῖνος ἐλέγξει τὸν κόσμον περὶ ἁμαρτίας καὶ περὶ δικαιοσύνης καὶ περὶ κρίσεως· ⁹ περὶ ἁμαρτίας μέν, ὅτι οὐ πιστεύουσιν εἰς ἐμέ· ¹⁰ περὶ δικαιοσύνης δέ, ὅτι πρὸς τὸν [e]πατέρα ὑπάγω καὶ οὐκέτι θεωρεῖτέ με· ¹¹ περὶ δὲ κρίσεως, ὅτι ὁ ἄρχων τοῦ κόσμου τούτου κέκριται. ¹² ”Ετι πολλὰ ἔχω [f]ὑμῖν λέγειν, ἀλλ' οὐ δύνασθε βαστάζειν ἄρτι· ¹³ ὅταν δὲ ἔλθῃ ἐκεῖνος, τὸ πνεῦμα τῆς ἀληθείας, ὁδηγήσει ὑμᾶς ἐν τῇ ἀληθείᾳ πάσῃ, οὐ γὰρ λαλήσει ἀφ' ἑαυτοῦ, ἀλλ' ὅσα [h]ἀκούσει λαλήσει, καὶ τὰ ἐρχόμενα ἀναγγελεῖ ὑμῖν. ¹⁴ ἐκεῖνος ἐμὲ δοξάσει, ὅτι ἐκ τοῦ ἐμοῦ λήμψεται καὶ ἀναγγελεῖ ὑμῖν. ¹⁵ πάντα ὅσα ἔχει ὁ πατὴρ ἐμά ἐστιν· διὰ τοῦτο εἶπον ὅτι ἐκ τοῦ ἐμοῦ λαμβάνει καὶ ἀναγγελεῖ ὑμῖν.

7 But I tell you the Truth, it is better for you that I go away. For if I do not go, the Paraclete will not come to you. And if I do go, I will send him to you. 8 And coming, that one will convince the world concerning sin and justice and judgment. 9 Concerning sin, because they did not believe in me; 10 and concerning justice, because I go to the Father and you no longer see me; 11 and concerning judgment, because the prince of this world has

been judged. 12 I have much more to say to you but you are not able to bear it now. 13 But when that one comes, the Spirit of Truth, he will guide you in all Truth, for he will not speak on his own, but what he hears he will speak, and announce the coming things to you. 14 That one will glorify me, because from me he will receive and announce it to you. 15 Everything that the Father has is mine. On account of this I said that he will receive from me and announce it to you.

We note that there are four occurrences of παράκλητος; four and only four. As they appear, so do the names of the Evangelists attached by early tradition to each text:

The prominent placement of words and highlighting individual letters within words was sometimes done to gesture toward the author's name as such. In Greek, Aratos opens his 1154 line didactic poem on the stars with a prominently displayed use of the adjective ἄρρητον/unspoken.[1] In Latin, a parade example of what I will call intercalation occurs in Vergil's Georgics. Like Aratus, Vergil discusses the moon and then embeds the first two letters of his trinomial PUblius VErgilius MAro (Georgics 1.428–32).[2]

The same is true of the Paraclete passages that embed into the Johannine text at the junctures pertinent to the respective Synoptic allusions the successive names attached to the Synoptics:

Μαθθαιος—(John 14:16,17)

²⁶ ὁ δὲ παράκλητος, τὸ πνεῦμα τὸ ἅγιον ὃ πέμψει ὁ πατὴρ ἐν τῷ ὀνόματί μου, ἐκεῖνος ὑμᾶς διδάξει πάντα καὶ ὑπομνήσει ὑμᾶς πάντα ἃ εἶπον ὑμῖν. ¹⁷ τὸ πνεῦμα τῆς ἀληθείας, ὃ ὁ κόσμος οὐ δύναται λαβεῖν, ὅτι οὐ θεωρεῖ αὐτὸ οὐδὲ γινώσκει· ὑμεῖς γινώσκετε αὐτό, ὅτι παρ' ὑμῖν μένει καὶ ἐν ὑμῖν ἔσται.

Μαρκος—(John 14:26)

²⁶ ὁ δὲ παράκλητος, τὸ πνεῦμα τὸ ἅγιον ὃ πέμψει ὁ πατὴρ ἐν τῷ ὀνόματί μου, ἐκεῖνος ὑμᾶς διδάξει πάντα καὶ ὑπομνήσει ὑμᾶς πάντα ἃ εἶπον ὑμῖν.

1. *Phaenomena* line 2
2. See Ross, *Backgrounds to Augustan Poetry*, 29.

Λουκας—(John 15:26)

²⁶ Ὅταν ἔλθῃ ὁ παράκλητος ὃν ἐγὼ πέμψω ὑμῖν παρὰ τοῦ πατρός, τὸ πνεῦμα τῆς ἀληθείας ὃ παρὰ τοῦ πατρὸς ἐκπορεύεται, ἐκεῖνος μαρτυρήσει περὶ ἐμοῦ·

Ιωαννης—(John 16:7–10a).

⁷ ἀλλ᾽ ἐγὼ τὴν ἀλήθειαν λέγω ὑμῖν, συμφέρει ὑμῖν ἵνα ἐγὼ ἀπέλθω. ἐὰν [a]γὰρ μὴ ἀπέλθω, ὁ παράκλητος]οὐ μὴ ἔλθῃ πρὸς ὑμᾶς· ἐὰν δὲ πορευθῶ, πέμψω αὐτὸν πρὸς ὑμᾶς.⁸ καὶ ἐλθὼν ἐκεῖνος ἐλέγξει τὸν κόσμον περὶ ἁμαρτίας καὶ περὶ δικαιοσύνης καὶ περὶ κρίσεως· ⁹ περὶ ἁμαρτίας μέν, ὅτι οὐ πιστεύουσιν εἰς ἐμέ· ¹⁰ περὶ δικαιοσύνης δέ, ὅτι πρὸς τὸν [a] πατέρα ὑπάγω καὶ οὐκέτι θεωρεῖτέ με·³

UNITY IN THE SPIRIT OF TRUTH

Note also that the phrase Spirit of Truth occurs explicitly at 15:26 and 16:13. "Spirit of Truth" follows immediately after the Paraclete passage in 14:16.

> John 14:17 τὸ πνεῦμα τῆς ἀληθείας, ὃ ὁ κόσμος οὐ δύναται λαβεῖν, ὅτι οὐ θεωρεῖ αὐτὸ οὐδὲ [y]γινώσκει· [z]ὑμεῖς γινώσκετε αὐτό, ὅτι παρ᾽ ὑμῖν μένει καὶ ἐν ὑμῖν [aa]ἔσται.
> The Spirit of Truth, whom the world is unable to receive, because it neither sees nor knows him. But you know him because he remains by you and is in you.

Three of the four Paraclete passages showcase the phrase Spirit of Truth. The remaining passage in John 14:26 may also be seen under that rubric. The Paraclete will remind the disciples of everything that Jesus has said to them. The popular etymology for a/ letheia is "not forgetting", an interesting simulacrum of Truth.

---

3. This allusion to John as author of the text stands in obvious tension with the allusion to Judas as author in John 21:24. I understand that tension under the umbrella of a phenomenon explored by Tom Geue who presents evidence for some authors in antiquity deliberately creating a sense of sometimes playful uncertainty about the identity of a textual author. See Geue, *Author Unknown*.

The four passages attend to alētheia, Truth, and are unified in such attention.

ESPECIALLY EMPHASIZED THEMES OF EACH GOSPEL IN THE PRESENT ORDERING OF THE PARACLETE SAYINGS

We might not then be totally surprised to find them unified in another way. The profile of the Paraclete traces special aspects of the texts that now surround the Fourth Gospel in their present canonical order.

Be with you

John 14:16 The Paraclete will be with you forever. See Matthew 1:23 Emmanuel, rendered 'God with us" as well as Matt 28:20

> "And behold, I am with you all days until the consummation of the Age."

Holy Teaching

Two themes are shared uniquely by the Paraclete saying in John 14:26 and Mark 1:23 –28—The Holy and teaching.

> John 14:26 The Paraclete will teach you. ²⁶ ὁ δὲ παράκλητος, τὸ πνεῦμα τὸ ἅγιον ὃ πέμψει ὁ πατὴρ ἐν τῷ ὀνόματί μου, ἐκεῖνος ὑμᾶς διδάξει πάντα καὶ ὑπομνήσει ὑμᾶς πάντα ἃ εἶπον ὑμῖν.
> And the Paraclete, the Holy Spirit, whom the Father will send in my Name will teach you everything and remind you of all that I have said to you ...

Alone among the Paraclete sayings is the Paraclete further described as the Holy Spirit. That approximates the assertion in Mark 1:24 that Jesus is also called the holy One of God.

Witness from the beginning

John 15:26 The Paraclete will witness concerning me. Immediately following is the statement that

> "you also will witness concerning me, because you are with me from the beginning ²⁷ καὶ ὑμεῖς δὲ μαρτυρεῖτε, ὅτι ἀπ' ἀρχῆς μετ' ἐμοῦ ἐστε. These same themes—witness /from the beginning—- bookend Luke. You are witnesses of these things (Luke 24:48) and the author's opening assertion that what he relates is what they who became eyewitnesses and servants of the word handed over to us from the beginning (Luke 1:2).

Forensic/didactic exploration of sin, justice, and judgment

Although the terms are not unique to John, their tight bundling in John 16:8–11 is. Since ἐλέγξει (John 16:8) is a forensic and didactic term, the Paraclete's convincing the world about the correct grasp of sin, justice and judgment seems to reflect the trial theme especially in John 5–10 in which Jesus embodies the Decalogue as he confronts resistance among some of his interlocutors.[4]

Guide

The next block of material John 16:12–15 has been seen by some commentators as a fifth arrangement of material, distinct from John 16:8–11. Schnackenburg is among them.[5] I draw our attention to the verb in Acts 8:31 "ὁδηγήσει-/guide" when the Ethiopian asks "How can I understand what I read unless someone guides me?" It is an extremely rare verb in the NT canon, occurring a total of only five times. Nearly all of the non-Johannine occurrences, whether noun or verb, use the term in a negative and

---

4. Beutler, A Commentary, 415—417. The trial to which Jesus subjects the world allows for both forensic and didactic dimensions.

5. Schnackenburg, *Gospel According to St. John*. 3.141–44.

ironic fashion. The Johannine instances (John 16:13 and Rev 7:17) are the exception. They are positive in import. I suggest that John 16:13 points to the verb "guide" in Acts 8:31, since they both treat exploration of the identity of Jesus as such; as the Truth in John 14; as the servant of Isaiah 53 in Acts 8.

Haenchen among others notes that both John and Acts display the respective authors' practice of separating words that would naturally belong together, listing several examples and referring to further studies already in print at the time.[6] I would take that observation one step further and emphasize its relevance to my thesis: The Johannine Paraclete sayings in John 16:8—11 that showcase the particularly forensic aspects of the Paraclete's actions are placed between the places where he alludes to Luke and Acts, i.e. John 15:26 and John 16:12-15.

These data present us then with connections between the Paraclete passages in John 14-16 and distinctive themes in the Synoptics and Acts.

THEMES ADJACENT TO PARACLETE SAYINGS AND REFLECTING THE GOSPELS AND ACTS

In addition, themes adjacent to those just mentioned in the various canonical Gospels and Acts inform the remarks of the Johannine author near the places expected. They are listed below *seriatim*, one through five. Note that the profile of Luke-Acts is raised in two distinct positions, John 16:1-4 and 16:12-15, serving different literary ends.

One

—John 14:21 commands
    Matthew—See Matthew 28:20
        teach them to observe all I have commanded you.

---

6. Haenchen. *John 1*, 1.62.

Two

—John 15: 2, 3—(un)clean
   Mark—See Mark 1:23-28 healing of a man with unclean spirit

Three

—John 16:4b

> these things I did not say to you because I was with you

This statement follows immediately upon one ["these things"] that could well describe the martyrdom of Stephen in Acts of the Apostles 8:1–3. Indeed, the words ἀπόστολοι/apostles and the name Στέφανος/Stephen are intercalated in John 16:2. If this verse alludes to that murder, it works together with the language of witness in John 15:26, 27 to respect the integrity of Luke—Acts as a document about witness to Jesus. I think that it also alludes to Luke- Acts as a known quantity prior to the creation of John.
   Luke—See Luke 24:44 My words that I spoke while I was with you.
   This statement focuses on Jesus' self-description in Luke that reflects the witness of Law, Prophets, and Psalms. Note that, insofar as John 16:4b focuses indirectly on what Jesus said in Luke, it is also congruent with the fact that the disciples in Luke in fact did not ask Jesus "Where are you going?" [thereby cohering with Jesus' claim in John 16:5].

Four

—John 16:8–11 convincing concerning sin, justice, judgment
   John—See John 5–10 in which Jesus in his person embodies aspects of the Decalogue

Five

—John 16:13-15 The verb ἀναγγελεῖ/announce, used three times in these three verses, brings us firmly into the realm of Acts of the Apostles. The verb occurs about the same number of times in John (6x) and Acts (5x) and far more than in any other canonical document of the canon as we know it. Its near-equivalent ἀπαγγελ- appears in John 16:25 and 14 times in Acts (more often than elsewhere in the emerging canon).

Acts of the Apostles—The verb ἀναγγελ- occurs at Acts 14:27, 15:4, 19:18, 20:20, 20:27.

The preponderant use of these verbs assumes the distinction of Acts from the Gospel of Luke and suggests a time when Luke precedes, and Acts follows, John.

SUMMARY OF DISTINCTIVE THEMES/ CANONICAL SEQUENCE

The following schema presents us with connections between the Paraclete passages in John 14-16 and distinctive themes in the Synoptics and Acts:

John 14:16—MATTHEW—Emmanuel/God with us; commands
John 14:26—MARK—holy, teaching and reminding; clean
John 15:26—LUKE-ACTS—witnesses from the beginning; what I did not say/said while I was with you
John 16:8—11—JOHN—the Paraclete's convincing the world about sin, justice and judgment; Jesus embodying the Decalogue in John 5—10
John 16:13—ACTS—guiding; the Spirit and Jesus will announce

THE REIGN OF GOD

This does not exhaust the range of questions relevant to the thesis. Among them are, for example, whether the content of the Johannine effort is intended to fill the gap created by the notice in Acts

1:3 that Jesus spent 40 days of post-resurrection life presenting the reign of God to the disciples. John 16:12–13 whose ὁδηγήσει we have already identified as pertinent to Acts of the Apostles 8:31, also intercalates the term for reign, βασιλεια.

¹² "Ἔτι πολλὰ ἔχω ὑμῖν λέγειν, ἀλλ' οὐ δύνασθε βαστάζειν ἄρτι· ¹³ ὅταν δὲ ἔλθῃ ἐκεῖνος, τὸ πνεῦμα τῆς ἀληθείας, ὁδηγήσει ὑμᾶς ἐν τῇ ἀληθείᾳ πάσῃ, οὐ γὰρ λαλήσει ἀφ' ἑαυτοῦ, ἀλλ' ὅσα ἀκούσει λαλήσει, καὶ τὰ ἐρχόμενα ἀναγγελεῖ ὑμῖν.

I have much to tell you, but you are unable to bear it now. When that one comes, the Spirit of Truth, he will guide you in all Truth, for he will not speak from himself, but what he will hear he will speak, and will announce the coming things to you.

CONCLUSIONS

The Fourth Evangelist's Paracletic descriptions draw on tradition, yes, as has been noted frequently in the scholarship. However, he is drawing on tradition in a particular order, that of the early portions of the canon as we know it today. Among the extant evidence, that sequence is not explicitly reflected by someone writing in his own voice until the Festal Letter of Bishop Athanasius of Alexandria in 367. Prior to that period, we have attestations of Origen's list of Matthew, Mark, Luke, John as reported by Eusebius (*Historia Ecclesiae* 6.25.4). Irenaeus knows the four texts in question, but follows the order suggested to him by the four living creatures of Rev 4:6–9. See Harry Gamble's study of the canon.[7]

One of the most interesting results of this approach to the Paraclete passages resides, I think, in The Evangelist's use of the intercalary dynamic already long-established in the wider tradition and in evidence in one of his near contemporaries, Valerius Flaccus and his *Argonautica*.[8]

7. Gamble, *New Testament Canon*. For more recent manuscript studies, see Hill and Kruger, *Early Text*.

8. Castelletti, "A "Greek" Acrostic," 319–23. Also see Carter, "*Vergilium*

This finding is a rather conservative one, admittedly. I am asserting that the Johannine author had a keen appreciation of his place among the emerging literature of the late 1st/early 2nd c. church, facilitated by relatively safe travel during the Pax Romana, even though it is one not reflected for centuries in our extant manuscript evidence. Should we say that he has provided us an index of sorts to part of the emerging canon of the early church?

Vestigare," 615–17.

Intercalated ἱλαστήριον/ Mercy Seat in John 19:13, 14

WHETHER PILATE SITS OR caused Jesus to sit in the Judgment Seat in this pericope continues to be debated.[1] However, the text may be read simply as "he (Pilate) led Jesus outside and he (Jesus) sat down." This is not a sensible reading if one considers routine treatment of the accused under Roman law, of course. However, Jesus sitting down may be a theological statement, affirming him as functioning in the context of the Mercy Seat of old. Intercalated subtext supports just such a reading of Jesus in the chair. The letters of ἱλαστήριον/Mercy Seat are sprinkled throughout these two verses and gesture toward a phenomenon in the Jewish Scriptures that provides a template behind the seat. Here are the letters:

¹³... Πιλᾶτος τῶν ... ἤγαγεν ...Λιθόστρωτον, Ἑβραϊστὶ ...
¹⁴ τοῦ ...]ἦν

Once a year, and only once a year, the high priest and only the High Priest, entered the divine presence at the Mercy Seat and sprinkled the structure with blood (Lev 16). The divine presence seated at the structure was asked to forgive and spare the people of Israel. Perhaps drawing on the occurrence of the Mercy Seat in Romans 3:25 and/or Hebrews 7–10, the Johannine Evangelist has Jesus sitting on the Judgment Seat and then led out to be crucified

1. Beutler, *Commentary*, 476.

INTERCALATED ἱλαστήριον/ MERCY SEAT IN JOHN 19:13, 14

where his blood is specifically singled out for attention (uniquely so among the canonical Gospels). We see the seating and handing over of Jesus best when we see it through the scrim of the Mercy Seat and blood offering.

Consider also the following intercalation:

The image of Jesus as ὁ ἀμνὸς τοῦ θεοῦ/ *the Lamb of God* resides in the letters of John

19:28, 29—

²⁸ ὁ . . . πάντα . . . ²⁹ . . . μεστόν· σπόγγον . . . μεστὸν τοῦ . . . περιθέντες προσήνεγκαν αὐτοῦ.

Let that be seen as a corollary of "The Lamb of God who takes away the sins of the world" (See John 1:29). While Lev 16:14 designates the blood of a *bull* in the ceremony at the Mercy Seat, the Evangelist has emphasized the blood of the Lamb in that capacity, perhaps partly influenced by the Servant's portrait in Isaiah 53.[2]

---

2. So Beutler, *Commentary*, 59.

Šemeš at the cross of Jesus (John 19:29)

²⁹ σκεῦος ἔκειτο ὄξους μεστόν· σπόγγον οὖν μεστὸν τοῦ ὄξους ὑσσώπῳ περιθέντες
προσήνεγκαν αὐτοῦ τῷ στόματι.
A jar full of sour wine stood (there) so they brought a sponge full of sour wine, surrounded by (a cluster of) hyssop, to his mouth.

THE SYNOPTIC PARALLELS OFFER a similar scenario, most closely in Mark 15:36. However, uniquely in John, the letters of ἕκτος/sixth are present ἔκειτο ὄξους surrounded by the Greek approximation of Hebrew šemeš/sun.

σκεῦος . . . μεστόν·

While still in conversation with Pilate, it was almost the sixth hour (19:14), that is, noon but now in 19:29 the intercalated presence of the sun would gesture more closely toward high noon, the sun at its observable apex. Lest the reader miss the gesture toward the sun, the μεσ·is repeated twice.

As the letters of sixth are surrounded by the letters of sun, so the sponge is surrounded by hyssop. The physical improbability of a single slip of hyssop capable of bearing up under the weight of a sponge makes a clump of the bush the more likely intended image.

Illumination and bush have their analogue in Exodus 3. Their presence there, as here in John 19, is accompanied by the explicit

ŠEMEŠ AT THE CROSS OF JESUS (JOHN 19:29)

or implicit revelation of I AM (Ex 3:14), fulfilling the promise of John's Jesus that "when you have lifted up the Child of Humanity, then you will know that I AM (John 8:28). From šemeš to šem, from sun to Name.

One is then perhaps not wholly surprised to find intercalated here in John 19:28–29 Ἐγώ εἰμι ὁ ὤν·/ I AM WHO AM (Exod 3:14):

[28] λέγει· Διψῶ. [29] σκεῦος ἔκειτο . . . μεστόν· περιθέντες προσήνεγκαν . . . ᾧ [30] . . . οὖν.

Afterword
Some Questions about Jacob Jordaens *The Four Evangelists*

DO THEY NOT ALL stand in the splendor of the breaking dawn celebrated by Mark? Do they occur in order of their appearance in the canon: Matthew on the left, Mark, Luke, John? One of Mark's hands lay over his heart but is the Alexandrian also prominently displaying the classic trope of a finger to the lips signaling awed silence amid meditation? They were doing this sort of thing in ancient Egyptian portraiture, also in the presence of books. Does Luke display three fingers in light to signal his place in the lineup? Does he get to hold the curtain open because of his determined attention to the skies? Does John display all five fingers to signal his place marking a break between four and five? Is the book in John's hand his Gospel or the Acts of the Apostles, the missing arm of Luke? Or does the bipartition of Luke's haircut limn the Gospel and Acts? Does the white beard elicit memory of Luke's preference for the old? Does the group study the Septuagint resting on the Hebrew text of the Jewish Scriptures? Is it the case that Matthew's left hand doesn't know what the right is doing? Is that a raven on his balding head? Has Mark now taken to wearing the radiant garment given him by the young man in the empty tomb? Does the color of Luke's nose suggest that he is an avid participant in dinner and drink with friends, like the Master? Is that an eagle feather in John's hand and the suggestion of the eagle beak in the fold of his cheek? Can we be sufficiently grateful to The Louvre Museum for preserving this treasure for the ages? And what thanks might we hope to render to Jacob Jordaens himself? Has *Henry V*, by intoning Psalm 113:9 Vulgate [Psalm 115:1 in The Revised Standard Version] said the most important thing in this regard: *Non nobis Domine, Domine; non nobis Domine. Sed nomini sed nomini tuo da gloriam.*

Bibliography

Abegg, Martin with Peter Flint and Eugene Ulrich, eds. *The Dead Sea Scrolls Bible: The Oldest Known Bible Translated for the First Time into English.* New York: Harper One, 1999.

Anacreon. In *Lyrica Graeca Selecta: Brevi Adnotatione Instruxit,* edited by D L Page, 153. Oxford: Oxford University Press:1968. rpt. with corrections 1976.

Aernie, Jeffrey W. "Cruciform Discipleship: The Narrative Function of the Women in Mark 15-16." *Journal of Biblical Literature* Vol. 135, No. 4 (Winter 2016) 779-97.

Apollonius of Rhodes. *Argonautica.* Edited and translated by William H. Race. Loeb Classical Library 1. Cambridge: Harvard University Press, 2008.

Aratus. *Phaenomena.* Edited with introduction, translation and commentary by Douglas Kidd. Cambridge Classical Texts and Commentaries 34. Cambridge: Cambridge University Press, 1997.

Aristophanes. *Aristophanes Acharnians Knights.* Edited and translated by Jeffrey Henderson. Loeb Classical Library. Cambridge: Harvard University Press, 1998. Rpt. with corrections 2018.

Beaton, Richard. *Isaiah's Christ in Matthew's Gospel.* Cambridge: Cambridge University Press, 2002.

——— "Messiah and Justice." *Journal for the Study of New Testament* 75 (1999) 5-23.

Beutler, Johannes. *A Commentary on the Gospel of John.* ET Grand Rapids: Eerdmans, 2017.

Blenkinsopp, Joseph. *Opening the Sealed Book: Interpretations of the Book of Isaiah in Late Antiquity.* Grand Rapids: Eerdmans, 2006.

Botticelli, Sandro. "Madonna of the Magnificat."

Brankaer, Johanna, ed., with an introduction by Bas van Os. *The Gospel of Judas.* Oxford: Oxford University Press, 2019.

Brown, Raymond E. *The Birth of the Messiah.* New York: Doubleday, 1977, 1993.

——— *An Introduction to the New Testament.* New York: Doubleday, 1997.

Bibliography

Burke, Tony. "Early Christian Apocrypha in Contemporary Theological Discourse." In *The Oxford Handbook of Early Christian Apocrypha,* edited by Andrew Gregory and Christopher Tuckett, 441-57. Oxford: Oxford University Press, 2015.

Burrell, David B. CSC. "Analogy, Creation, and Theological Language." In *The Theology of Thomas Aquinas,* edited by Rik van Niewenhove and Joseph Wawrykow, 77-98. South Bend, IN: University of Notre Dame, 2005.

Carne-Ross, D.S. *Pindar.* New Haven: Yale, 1985.

Carter, Matthew A.S. "*Vergilium Vestigare: Aeneid 12.587-88.*" *Classical Quarterly* 2002. Vol. 52. Issue 2. 615-17.

Cary, Earnest. *Dionysus.* "Excerpts: *19. 5, 1-4*" also designated as 17,7; 2,3." In *Roman Antiquities Book XI. Fragments of Books XII-XX.* Loeb Classical Library VII, Cambridge, MA: Harvard University Press, 1950.

Castelletti, C. "A 'Greek' Acrostic in Valerius Flaccus (3.430-34)." *Mnemosyne* 65 (2012) 319-23.

Charlesworth, James H. *The Beloved Disciple.* Valley Forge: Trinity, 1995.

Collins, Adela Yarbro. Edited by Harold W. Attridge. *Mark: A Commentary.* Hermeneia Series. Minneapolis: Fortress, 2007.

F H Colson and G H Whitaker. *Philo. Allegorical Interpretation of Genesis 2, 3.* Loeb Classical Library 226. Cambridge: Harvard University Press, 1929.

Dell, Katharine J. "The Suffering Servant of Deutero-Isaiah: Jeremiah Revisited." In *Genesis, Isaiah and Psalms: A Festschrift to Honor Professor John Emerton for His Eightieth Birthday,* edited by Adney Emerton et al., 119-34. Leiden: Brill 2010.

Dionysus. "Excerpts: 19. 5, 1-4" also designated as 17,7; 2,3." *Roman Antiquities Book XI. Fragments of Books XII-XX.* Translated by Earnest Cary. Loeb Classical Library, Cambridge, MA: Harvard University Press, 1950.

Dodd, C H. *Historical Tradition in the Fourth Gospel.* Cambridge: Cambridge University Press, 1963. rpt. 1978.

Duhm, Bernhard. *Das Buch Jesaja* 4th ed. HKAT 3/1. Goettingen: Vandenhoek & Ruprecht, 1922.

Edwards M J. *Quoting Aratus: Acts 17, 28. Zeitschrift der Neutestamentliche Wissenschaft* Jan. 1, 1992; 83 Periodicals Archive Online, 266-79.

Fitzmyer, Joseph A. *1 Corinthians.* New Haven and London: Yale University Press, 2008.

———*The Gospel According to Luke I-IX.* Anchor Bible volumes 28 and 29 New York: Doubleday, 1981.

Fowler, Harold North. *Plato. Phaedo.* In *Euthyphro Apology Crito Phaedo Phaedrus.* Loeb Classical Library 36. Cambridge: Harvard University Press, 1914. Rpt. 1995.

Franke, John R. *Joshua, Judges, Ruth, 1-2 Samuel* in Thomas Oden, gen. ed. *Ancient Christian Commentary on Scripture* vol. 4. Downers Grove: IVP, 2005.

Gamble, Harry Y. *The New Testament Canon: Its Making and Meaning.* Philadelphia: Fortress, 1985.

BIBLIOGRAPHY

Geue, Tom. *Author Unknown: The Power of Anonymity in Ancient Rome.* Cambridge, MA: Harvard University Press, 2019.

Greenstein, Edward L. *Job: A New Translation.* New Haven: Yale University Press, 2019.

Griffin, C S. *Judas Iscariot: The Author of the Fourth Gospel.* Boston: Scot-Parkin Printing Co., 1892.

Gutzwiller, Kathryn. "Literary Criticism." In *A Companion to Hellenistic Literature,* edited by James J. Clauss and Martine Cuypers, 337– 65. Wiley Blackwell 2014.

Haenchen, Ernst. *John 1: A Commentary on the Gospel of John. Chapters 1–6. John 2: A Commentary on the Gospel of John. Chapters 7–21. English Translation* Philadelphia: Fortress, 1984.

Harris, J. Rendel. "On the Alternative Ending of St. Mark's Gospel." *Journal of Biblical Literature* Vol. 12, No. 2 (1893) 96–103.

Harvey, Bruce J. *Yhwh Elohim: A Survey of Occurrences in the Leningrad Codex and Their Corresponding Septuagintal Renderings.* New York: Clark, 2011.

Heim, Maximilian Heinrich. *Joseph Ratzinger: Life in the Church and Living Theology.* San Francisco: Ignatius, 2007.

Henderson, Jeffrey. *Aristophanes Acharnians Knights.* Loeb Classical Library. Cambridge: Harvard University Press, 1998. Rpt. with corrections 2018.

Hill, Charles E. and Michael J. Kruger, eds. *The Early Text of the New Testament.* Oxford: Oxford University Press, 2012.

Holladay, Carl R. "Jesus' Ministry in Galilee in Matthew 8–10." In *Gospel Images of Jesus Christ in Church Tradition and in Biblical Scholarship,* edited by Christos Karakolis, Karl-Wilhelm Niebuhr and Sviatoslav Rogalsky, 313–36. Tubingen: Mohr Siebeck, 2012.

Hutchinson, G. O. *Greek Lyric Poetry: A Commentary on Selected Larger Pieces.* Oxford: Oxford University Press, 2001.

Irenaeus. *Against Heresies.* In *Ante-Nicene Fathers. Vol. 1 The Apostolic Fathers, Justin Martyr, Irenaeus,* edited by Alexander Roberts and James Donelson, 307–567. Peabody, MA: Hendrickson, 1994.

Iverson, Kelly R. "A Further Word on Final Γαρ (Mark 16:8)." *Catholic Biblical Quarterly* Vol. 68, No. 1 (January 2006) 79–94.

Jones, Horace Leonard. *The Geography of Strabo II. Books 15–16.* Loeb Classical Library 241. Cambridge: Harvard University Press, 1930. Rpt. 2000.

Kaufmann, Yehezkel. *The Babylonian Captivity and Deutero-Isaiah.* New York: Union of the Hebrew Congregations of New York, 1970.

Keener, Craig. *The Gospel of John: A Commentary.* 2 Vols. Peabody, MA: Hendrickson, 2003.

Kidd, Douglas. *Aratus. Phaenomena.* Cambridge Classical Texts and Commentaries 34. Cambridge: Cambridge University Press, 1997.

Kiley, Mark C. "Johannine Discipleship." *The Bible Today* March/April (2008) 87—92.

———"The Latinity of Johannine Witness." In *Gospel Essays: Frontier of Sacred and Secular,* 40–57. Eugene, OR: Wipf & Stock, 2012.

BIBLIOGRAPHY

———"Matthew's Pi." In *Gospel Essays: Frontier of Sacred and Secular*, 1–13. Eugene, OR: Wipf & Stock, 2012.

———"Why 'Matthew' in Matt 9, 9–13?" *Biblica* 1984 Vol. 65 No. 3 (1984) 347–51.

Kim, Lawrence. "Figures of Silence in Dio Chrysostom's First Tarsian Oration (Oration 33): Aposiopesis, Paraleipsis, and Huposiopesis." *Greece & Rome*, Vol. 60, No. 1, © The Classical Association, 2013. 32–49.

Knox, Wilfrid Lawrence. "The Ending of St. Mark's Gospel." *Harvard Theological Review* Vol. 35, No. 1 (Jan. 1942) 13–23.

Layton, Bentley. *The Gnostic Scriptures*. Garden City, NY: Doubleday, 1987.

Levine, Amy-Jill and Marc Zvi Brettler. *The Bible With and Without Jesus: How Jews and Christians Read the Same Stories Differently*. New York: Harper, 2020.

———"Pharisees in Luke." In *The Jewish Annotated New Testament*, edited by Amy-Jill Levine and Marc Zvi Brettler. 2nd ed. 122. Oxford: Oxford University Press, 2017.

Lincoln, Andrew T. "The Promise and the Failure: Mark 16:7, 8." *Journal of Biblical Literature* Vol. 108, No. 2 (Summer 1989) 283–300.

Lloyd-Jones, Hugh. *Sophocles. Oedipus at Colonus*. In *Antigone Women of Trachis Philoctetes Oedipus at Colonus*. Loeb Classical Library 21. Cambridge: Harvard University Press, 1994. Rpt. with Corrections 1998.

Lyons, Michael. "Psalm 22 and the 'Servants' of Isaiah 54; 56–66." *Catholic Biblical Quarterly* 77 no. 4 (Oct. 2015) 640–66.

Marcus, Joel. *Mark 1–8*. New Haven: Yale Anchor Bible, 2000.

Miller, Frank Justus. *Ovid Metamorphoses Books IX–XV*. Revised by G. P. Goold. Cambridge: Harvard University Press, 1984.

Minnis, Alastair J. "Figuring the Letter: Making Sense of *sensus litteralis* in Late Medieval Christian Exegesis." In *Interpreting Scriptures in Judaism, Christianity, and Islam: Overlapping Inquiries*, edited by Mordechai Z. Cohen and Adele Berlin, 159–82. Cambridge: Cambridge Univ. Press, 2016.

Moulton, James Hope and W F Howard. *A Grammar of New Testament Greek* Vol. I. *Prolegomena*. 3rd edition. Edinburgh: Clark. 1908. Rpt. 1957.

Noack, Ludwig. *Aus der Jordanwege nach Golgata: Die Geschichte Jesu auf Grund freier geschichtlicher Untersuchungen uber das Evangelium und die Evangelien*. Mannheim: Schneider, 1876.

North, Christopher R. *The Suffering Servant in Deutero-Isaiah: An Historical and Critical Study*. Oxford: Oxford University Press, 1948.

O'Grady, Paul. "Philosophical Theology and Analytical Philosophy in Aquinas." In *The Theology of Thomas Aquinas*, edited by Rik van Niewenhove and Joseph Wawrykow. 416–41. South Bend, IN: University of Notre Dame, 2005.

Overbeck, Franz. *Das Johanesevengelium: Studien zur Kritik und seiner Erforschung*. Tuebingen: Mohr, 1911.

Ovid. *Metamorphoses* Books 9-15. Translated by Frank Justus Miller. Revised by GP Goold. Loeb Classical Library 43. Cambridge: Harvard University Press, 1984.

Page, D.L. ed. *Lyrica Graeca Selecta: Brevi Adnotatione Instruxit.* Oxford: Oxford University Press:1968. rpt. with corrections 1976.

Pagels, Elaine and Karen L. King. *Reading Judas: The Gospel of Judas and the Shaping of Christianity.* New York: Viking, 2007.

Parke-Taylor, G.H. *Yahweh: The Divine Name in the Bible.* Waterloo, Ont.: Waterloo Univ. Press, 1975.

Paul, Shalom M. *Isaiah 40-66 Translation and Commentary.* Grand Rapids; Eerdmans, 2012.

Perrin, Bernadotte. *Plutarch. Parallel Lives. Demosthenes and Cicero. Alexander and Caesar.* Loeb Classical Library 99. Cambridge: Harvard University Press, 1919.

Philo. *Allegorical Interpretation of Genesis 2, 3.* Translated by F H Colson and G H Whitaker. Loeb Classical Library 226. Cambridge: Harvard University Press, 1929.

Plato. *Phaedo.* In *Euthyphro Apology Crito Phaedo Phaedrus.* Translated by Harold North Fowler. Loeb Classical Library 36. Cambridge: Harvard University Press, 1914. Rpt. 1995.

Plutarch. *Parallel Lives. Demosthenes and Cicero. Alexander and Caesar.* Loeb Classical Library 99. Translated by Bernadotte Perrin. Cambridge: Harvard University Press, 1919.

Race, William H. Editor and Translator. *Apollonius of Rhodes. Argonautica.* Loeb Classical Library 1. Cambridge: Harvard University Press, 2008.

Rahner, Karl. "The Immaculate Conception." In *Theological Investigations.* Vol. 1. 201-14. Baltimore: Helicon, 1961. rpt. 1969.

Roberts, Alexander and James Donelson, eds. *Ante-Nicene Fathers. Vol. 1. The Apostolic Fathers, Justin Martyr, Irenaeus* (Peabody, MA: Hendrickson, 1994).

Rosel, Martin. "Names of God." In *Encyclopedia of the Dead Sea Scrolls,* edited by Lawrence H. Schiffman and James C. VanderKam, 600-602. Oxford: Oxford University Press, 2000.

Ross, David O. *Backgrounds to Augustan Poetry. Cambridge:* Cambridge Univ. Press, 1975.

Sanders, E. P. "Testament of Abraham." In *The Old Testament Pseudepigrapha.* Two volumes, edited by James H. Charlesworth. 1.871-902. Garden City, NY: Doubleday, 1983, 1985.

Schnackenburg, Rudolf. *The Gospel According to St. John.* New York: Crossroad, 1987. Three volumes.

Schneiders, Sandra M. IHM "The Resurrection (of the Body) in the Fourth Gospel." In *Life in Abundance: Studies of John's Gospel in Tribute to Raymond E. Brown,* edited by John R. Donahue SJ., 168-98. Collegeville: Liturgical, 2005.

BIBLIOGRAPHY

Schiffman, Lawrence H. "Pharisees." In *The Jewish Annotated New Testament*, edited by Amy-Jill Levine and Mark Zvi Brettler, 619-22. 2nd ed. Oxford: 2017.

Schmidt, Michael. *The First Poets: Lives of the Ancient Greek Poets*. New York: Knopf, 2005.

Seltman, Charles. *The Twelve Olympians*. New York: Thomas Y. Crowell, 1960.

Shepherd, Charles E. *Theological Interpretation of Isaiah 53: A Critical Comparison of Bernhard Duhm, Brevard Childs, and Alec Motyer*. New York: Bloomsbury/ Clark, 2014.

Soon, Isaac T. "The Little Messiah: Jesus as τη ηλικια μικρος in Luke 19:3." *Journal of Biblical Literature* Vol. 142 no. 1, 2023. 151–70.

Sophocles. *Oedipus at Colonus*. In Antigone Women of Trachis Philoctetes Oedipus at Colonus. Loeb Classical Library 21. Edited and translated by Hugh Lloyd-Jones. Cambridge: Harvard University Press, 1994. Rpt. with Corrections 1998.

Strabo. *The Geography of Strabo II*. Books 15-16. Translated by Horace Leonard Jones. Loeb Classical Library 241. Cambridge: Harvard University Press, 1930. Rpt. 2000.

Suggs, M. Jack. "Wisdom of Solomon 2:10—5:23. A Homily Based on the Fourth Servant Song." *Journal of Biblical Literature* 76, 1 (March 1957) 26–33.

Tanner, Kathryn. "Self-Critical Cultures and Divine Transcendence." In *Theology After Liberalism: A Reader*, edited by John Webster and George P. Schner, 223–56. Malden, MA: Blackwell, 2000.

Taylor, Vincent. *The Gospel According to Saint Mark: The Greek Text with Introduction, Notes, and Indexes*. 2nd edition. Grand Rapids: Baker, 1966.

Tillich, Paul. *Systematic Theology: Three Volumes in One*. Chicago: Univ. of Chicago Press, 1967. 3.300-423.

Turner, Nigel *Grammar of New Testament Greek* Vol. IV. Edinburgh: Clark, 1972.

Van der Horst, Pieter. "Can a Book End with gar?: A Note on Mark XVI.8." *The Journal of Theological Studies* 01/01/1972. Volume 23. Issue 1. 121–24.

Volk, Katherina. "*Letters in the Sky: Reading the Signs in Aratus'* Phaenomena." *American Journal of Philology* 133 (2012) 209–40.

Wilkinson, Robert. *Tetragrammaton: Western Christians and the Hebrew Name of God from the Beginnings to the Seventeenth Century*. Leiden: Brill, 2015.

Ancient Document Index

OLD TESTAMENT/ HEBREW BIBLE

Genesis

Reference	Page
1	82
1:22, 28	111
3	45
3:1	45
3:15	43, 45, 46
3:15b	44
11:10–32	68
11:27—25:10	50, 80
11:31	69
12	69
12:5	69
12:9	69
12–25	61
12:1–13	58
14:17–20	74
14:17	74
14:18	74
14:19, 20	74
14:19	58
14:20	58, 74
15:1–5	63
15:5	52, 56, 69, 70, 73
15:9	53
17:10	69
17:11	69
17:14	69
18:1–8	63
18:6–8	79
18:6	75
18:7	75
18:8	79
18:1–19	75
18:13	75
18:19	75
18:20–21	73
18:32	72
19	73, 75, 77
19:1	77
19:28	77
19:30–35	59
20:5	72
21:8	70
21:10	71
21:14–16	69
21:14	69, 78
21:16	78
21:20	64, 71
22	59
22:7	78
22:10	69
22:13	78
22:17	54, 59, 74
50:24	82

Ancient Document Index

Exodus

1	2
3:2	23
3:14	39
3:14 LXX	84
3	148
3:14	23, 149
16	24, 25, 26, 30, 38
16 and 17	27
16:12	24, 38
16:15	24, 38, 96
16:21	26
17	85

Leviticus

1:1	2
16	146
16:14	147
20:24	56

Numbers

13:30	20
14:24	20

Deuteronomy

6	48
6:4	5
6	48
8	85
8:15	86
21:20	48
29:4	131
33: 18, 19	100

Joshua

7:1, 16–18	100
15:16–17	20

Judges

1:12–13	20

1 Samuel

18:4	97
20:2	97
20:39	97

2 Samuel

12	94
12:1–5	91, 93
19:19	101

1 Kings

19	39
19:12	30, 39

2 Kings

1–13	7

1 Chronicles

1 Chron 12:33	100

Job

Job 29:3	28
Job 29:4	28, 29
Job 29:9	28
Job 29:12 LXX	29
Job 29:16 LXX	29
Job 29:17	28

Psalms

22	11
2	33
8:6	123
21:10 LXX	33
2:10, 11 LXX	37
2:12 LXX	33
21:15 LXX	36
21:23, 26 LXX	33
21:26 LXX	37
21:29 LXX	33
21:32 LXX	36, 37
22	33

Ancient Document Index

22:1	33
41:6	108
85 LXX	76
103:4	123
109 LXX	38
109:1–3	38
109:1 LXX	35
109:3 LXX	35, 36
109: 3, 4 LXX	34
109:5,6	35
109:7 LXX	37
110	33
110:1	33
117 LXX	33, 34, 36, 37, 38
117:19 LXX	36
117:19, 20 LXX	35
117: 21–23 LXX	36
117:22 LXX	34, 35
117: 22–23 LXX	37
118	33
118:25, 26	33

Song of Solomon

3:4	91, 117, 118

Isaiah

6	65, 83
7:14	1
10:30	6
28:23	6
29:10	131
29:13 LXX	17
34:1	6
37–39	7
40:10	104
40:22	63
42, 49, 50, 52–53	7
42–49	6
42	6, 8
42:1–4	3, 4, 5, 9
42:8	7
49–50	6
49–53	6
49:1–6	4, 5
49:1	6
49:6	83
50	8
50:4	26
50:4–9	4, 5
50:10	7
52:13—53:12	5, 9
53	141, 147
54:5	7
65:13, 14	10
65:15	10

Jeremiah

31:15	2
50	91, 102
50: 16, 19	102
50:34	102

Lamentations

3	8
5:16	8

Daniel

12:6	31
12:9	31

Hosea

11:1	2

Amos

8:11–12	26

Micah

5:1	2

APOCRYPHA

Wisdom of Solomon

2:10—5:23	8
10:21—11:9	85, 86
11:4	86
11:6	86
11:6–8	86
11:8, 9	86
11:22	104
11:22–23	104

2 Maccabees

7:33	81

NEW TESTAMENT

Matthew

1:1	1
1:18	1
1:18–25	1
1:23	139
2:1–12	2
2:11	2
2:6	2
2:13–15	2
2:16–18	3
2:16	2
2:18	3
2:19–23	3
2:23	3
3:6	75
4–12	3, 4, 8
4, 8, 9, 12	9, 10
4:23–25	9
7:12—	1
8:8	13
8:23–34	10
9 and 15	17
9:25, 26	17
9:27–31	10
9: 35, 36	9
10:5, 6	13
12:18–21	9
12:21	9
13:27, 28	12
13:30	112, 115, 116
13:43	112
14:2	12
14:20	14
15	17
15:19	17
15:37	14
18:23	12
19:9	14
19:10–12	14
21: 34, 35, 36	12
22: 3,4,6,8,10,13	12
24:28	73
24:43–45	50
25:14, 19	12
26:58	12
27	108
27:3	99
27:5	108
28	13
28:20	139, 141

Mark

1	22, 33
1 and 8	25
1–8	27
1–9	23
1:1	33
1:5	75
1:11	33
1:15, 21–28	95
1:21	27
1:23–28	139, 142
1:23	96
1:24	139
1:26	96
1:27	27, 96
1:35–37	25, 27
1:35	26, 27
1:35–39	26

Ancient Document Index

1:37	26	9	23
1:38	25, 26	9:1–13	29
1:43	41	9:3	23
1:44	39	9:3,4	23
1:45	41	9:5	29
1–15	30, 32	9:3	29
3	116	9:5	29
3:35	124	9:9	29
5–7	16	9:14–29	29
5:3—7:30	18	9:18	28
5:35	16	9:22	29
5:38	16	9:22–23, 28–29	29
5:43	17	9:25	29
6:1–6	25	9:47, 49	22, 23
6:15, 48	39	10: 4, 5	26
6:31	25	11	33
6:45–52	16	11:9	33
7	20, 22	12	33
7:4	21	12:36	33
7: 6, 7	17	13:32	38
7:1–30	21	14	27
7:14–23	19	14:22, 23	27
7:19–21	19	15	27, 33
7:24–30	19, 20	15:26, 27	27
7:14–30	20	15:34	33
7:21–23	17, 18	15:36	148
7:28	26	15:40	33
7:31–33	17, 18	15:40, 47	33
7:31	27	16	30, 38, 40
7:31–37	18	16:1	30, 32
7:32–34	22	16:1–8	30, 38
7:32	83	16:2	34, 38
7:33	22	16:2a	38
7:34, 35	18	16:2b	38
7:36	17	16:2–4	38
8	22, 25	Mark 16:3–5	35
8:10	24, 25, 27	Mark 16:3	34
8:22–26	27	Mark 16:4	35
8: 23–26	23, 83	Mark 16:5	35
8:23	22	Mark 16:6	36, 39, 40, 41
8:24–25	23	Mark 16:6, 7	39
8:28 and 9:22	39	Mark 16:7	36, 37, 40, 41
8: 29, 30, 33	83	Mark 16: 7, 8	31, 32, 40
8:31–38	18	Mark 16:8	37, 41

Luke

1 and 2	66, 121
1	50, 51, 54, 55, 66
Eighth word, Luke 1:1	54
1:1	55
1:1, 2	54
1:5	55
1:34–38	121
1:36, 38, 39–41	66
1:37	75
1:37, 38	55
1:38	122
1:39	55
1:42	121
1:45	122
1:48	122
1:49	122
1:55, 72–74	55
1:66	65
2:3,4	66
2:3, 48	66
2:4	66
2:7	67
2:7, 15	67
2:8	67
2:8,9	67
2:15	121
2:20	68
2:22	67, 68
2:25,26	67
2:29,30	68
2:30	121
2:34	68
2:36	66
2:50	121
2:52	68
3	75, 78
3:1–20	58
3:6	58
3:23–38	68
3:38	48
4:12	68
4:20–23, 25,26	69
6:48, 49	76
7	46, 48
7:1	69
7:2	69
7:3	69
7:3,4	69
7:7,8	69
7:9,10	69
7:16	82
7:32–34	69
7:33	69
7:34	48
7:36–50	48
7:36	45
7:39	47
7:39, 40a	46
7:40, 41	47
7:41, 42	47
7:41b–42	46
7:44	47
7:44a	46
7:50	47
8:1,2	69
8:8	54
8:25	65
9:2	110
9:9	69
9:28, 29	69
9:31	82
9:2	110
9:62	112, 114, 115
10:17–20	70
10:17, 18	70
10:21	70
10:23	70
10:26	50
10: 34, 35	70
10:54	70
11:20,21,22	66
11:27,28	70
11:48	65
12:1–3	70
12:13–21	71
12:13	71

ANCIENT DOCUMENT INDEX

12:15	71	20:37, 38	74
12:39	50, 71	22	63, 75, 78
12:42	65	22:23	65
12:49	71	22:24-30, 35-38	75
12... 54	70	22:25, 26	75
13:10-17	71	22:26	75
13:11	71	22:27	75
13:12, 13	71	22:28	75
13:15	71	22:30	127
13:28	72	22:36, 37, 38	75
13:31	87	22:37, 38	77
16:25-26	72	22:41	77
17:11-19	72	22:42	77
17:11	72	22:43, 44	76, 77
17:17	72	23	46, 48
17:28-32	73	23:8	78
17:34-37	73	23:25	77
17:34	73	23:26	78
17:35	73	23:27	78
17:37	72, 73	23:28	78
18:1, 2	73	23:29	78
18:13	72	23:30	78
19	82	23:31	78
19:2	74	23:33, 34b	46
19:2, 8	74	23:34a	76
19:3	73	23:35a	46
19:5	73	23:47	78
19:8	74	23:47, 49, 50	78
19:9	73	23:48, 49	78
19:11-40	74	23:50, 51	77
19:10, 11	81	23:51, 52	79
19:11	74	24	46, 79
19:15-16	74	24:1	77
19:17	74	24:31	79
19:23-26	74	24:37-39	83
19:27, 28	74	24:39	83
19:35b-37a	81	24:42	79
19:37-40	74	24:29,30	79
19:42	82	24:44	76, 142
19:44	81, 82	24:51	80
20:9-19	74	24:52	80
20:19	74		

John

1 and 2	123
1	92
1:38, 41, 42; 20:16	112
1 and 20	112
1:13	122
1:29	129, 147
2	116
2:11	127
3:3, 5	118
4:10	97
4:14	86
5–10	140, 142
5	101, 105
5:5	101
6, 13, 21	101
6	94, 95, 98, 109, 118
6:15	95
6:19	95
6:22	101
6:31	96
6:37	96
6:42	96
6:45	96
6:47	95
6:51	95
6:59	96
6:60	95
6:70	96, 101, 127
7	85, 87
7:7–10	87
7:10	87
7:15	85
7:22–24	87
7:30	109
7:37–39	85, 86, 87
7:37	86
7:38	85, 86
7:42	94
8:1–11	133, 134
8:4, 5	133
8:6	133
8:7–9	134
8:9, 10	134
8:20	109
8:28	149
10:15, 17, 18 (bis)	117
11:29	101
12	108
12 and 13	94, 108
12:6	93
13–17	89
13	88, 92, 100, 101, 102, 105, 106, 126
13 and 18	126
13:1	101
13:2	100, 126,
13:4	97
13:4–20	101
13:12	122
13:16	122
13:17	122
13:19	122
13:24	88
13:27	101
13:2, 11	88
13:21	90
13:25	126
13:26–28	88
13:33	94
13:37, 38	117
13 and 20	91, 101
13 and 18	97
13:2	127
13:25	127
14–16	120, 121, 141, 143
14	141
14:12–14	121
14:13	97, 121
14:16	135, 138, 139, 143
14:16, 17	137
14:17	138
14:21	141

Ancient Document Index

14:26	135, 136, 137, 138, 139, 143	19:13, 14	146
15:2, 3	142	19:14	148
15:5, 8	121	19: 25–30	127
15:15	121	19: 26, 27	117, 123
15:7, 8	121	19:26–28a	124
15:13	117	19:28, 29	147, 149
15:15	97	19:29	148
15:16	121	19:31–37	123
15:17	121	19:34	123
15:26	135, 136, 138, 140, 141, 143	20	99, 102
		20:4	101
15: 26, 27	142	20:8	118
16:1–4	141	20:11–18	119
16:4b	142	20:11, 12	119
16:5	142	20:23	119
16:7–10a	138	20:23a	119
16:7–15	136	20:23b	119
16:8	140	20:29	119
16:8–11	135, 136, 140, 141, 42, 143	20:31	105
		21	91, 100, 102, 103, 106, 107, 112
16:12–15	135, 140, 141		
16:12–13	144	21:2	106
16:13	138, 141	21: 2, 3	111
16:13–15	143	21:3b–4a	101
16:15--22	121	21:7	102, 111
16:23	121	20, 21	99, 109
16:25	143	21:1–14	91, 110
16:26	121	21:15–22	113
16:29–32	121	21:20–25	106
17:1	105	21:20	102, 104
17:12	99	21:22, 23	118
17–21	102	21:22	102, 105, 108, 115, 116
18	98, 99, 100, 126	21:23	102
18:4, 5	100, 115	21:24	88, 89, 103, 105
18:8b	99		
18:10, 11	99	21:1w–14	109
18:15	101	21:11	106
19	148	21:20–23	107
19–21	123	21:22	107
19	99, 119	21:24	103, 107, 138

Acts of the Apostles

1:2–16	56
1:1a, b	80
1:3	144
1:11	55
1:12	56
1:12–16	56
1:13–15	56
1:13	56
1:14	56
1:15	56
1:18	108
1:22	100
2:1	56
3:1–10	57
3:1	56, 57
3:1, 2	58
3:6	57
3:9	57
3:10	56
3:11–26	57
3:13	57
3:14	58
3:16	57
3:17, 18	57
3:18–20	57
3:19	58
3:21	82
5	58
5: 1–11	58
5:3, 4	58
6:1, 7	58
6:2	64
6:5	64
6–8	59
6:8	59
6:11, 12	59
8	141
8:1–3	142
8:31	140, 144
8:3	59
8:22	55
8:26–40	59
8:26	59
8:27	59, 61
8:32	59
8:33b	61
8:32, 33	83
8:40	59, 60
9, 22, 26	109
9	60, 62
9:3	60, 82
9:4, 5	60
9:5	60
9:8w–10	60
9:18	60
9:36- 43	61
9:36, 37	61
9:38	61
9:39	60, 61
9:40	60, 61
9:41	60
11:18	55
12:7	61
12:18	55
12:21	61
12:22	61
13:2,11,26,40,41	61
13:38	61
14:8, 12	62
14:27	143
15	62
15:4	143
15: 7,12,13,14	62
16:1—18:17	62
16:12, 13	62
16:13	143
16: 16–28	62
17	50, 51,52, 63
17:18	53
17:22a	53
17:23	52
17:24	52
17:27	51, 55
17:28	52
17:29–30	52
17:30	61
17:34	53

Ancient Document Index

18	63
18:1–6	62, 63
18: 1, 2	63
18: 4–6	63
19:18	143
20: 7–12	63
20:11	63
20:20	143
20:27	143
21: 7, 8, 9	64
21:11	64
21:13	64
21:38	55
26:12, 13	64
26:12–18	64
26:14	64
26:14, 15	65
26:18	65
26:23	82
27	60
27: 1, 3	65
27:20	65
27: 34, 44	60
27:43, 44	65
28:2, 3	65
28:16, 17	65
28: 24, 25	83
28: 26, 27	65, 83
Acts 28:30, 31	55

Romans

3:25	57, 146
3:25c	61
5	48
8:26	48
9–11	78, 102
9:27	103
10	91, 102
10:9	103
11	103
11:8	131
11:17–24	78
11:26	103, 131
16:16	48

16:19	47
16:19, 20	48
16:20a	46

1 Corinthians

2: 7, 8, 12	40
10:4	85, 87
11	103
11:23–26	103
15	62
15: 3, 4	123
15:4	39
15:25	124

Galatians

1:4a	123
3:26–28	13

Colossians

1:13	106
1:15–20	80
1:20	81
3:3	40, 106
4:11	107

Hebrews

7–10	146

1 John

4:10	126
5:16, 17	125

Jude

3	126 127
17	126
18	127
20	127
20, 21	126
22, 23	126
23	126

Revelation

4:6–9	144
7:17	141
19:12	127
21:14	127

DEAD SEA SCROLLS

1QIs-a	5

GRECO-ROMAN WRITINGS

Anacreon	68
Apollonius *Argonautica* 4.783–90	18
Aratos, *Phaenomena*	
Eighth word, Ph 2	54
Ph 2	137
Ph 3–5	51
Ph 5	52
Ph 5–14	54
Ph 21–27	66, 80
Ph 35–44	65
Ph 60–70	77
Ph 78–79	56
Ph 96–139	58
Ph 132	58
Ph 147–78	66
Ph 148	67
Ph 167, 168	67
Ph 97	56
Ph 147	66
Ph 177–78	68
Ph 198	60
Ph 201	61
Ph 203	60, 61
Ph 204	60
Ph 205–24	60
Ph 220	62
Ph 221	60
Ph 235	65
Ph 257–58	64
Ph 267	64
Ph 269, 275	62
Ph 300–310	64
Ph 300w –302	71
Ph 304–5	64
Ph 306	64
Ph 313–15	73
Ph 326	74
Ph 326–37	73
Ph 358–61	62
Ph 369–70	72
Ph 408–10	52
Ph 408	53
Ph 408–10	53
Ph 427	60, 70
Ph 454–61	79
Ph 470–79	55
Ph 476	69
Ph 507–23	72
Ph 543	72
Ph 570–74	71
Ph 572–76	59
Ph 587–88	57
Ph 588–89	75, 76
Ph 600	62
Ph 617–21	63
Ph 754	57
Ph 892, 898	65
Ph 892–98	71
Ph 898	68
Ph 913	61
Ph 914–15	61
Ph 995	65
Ph 1013–18	65
Ph 1028–30	55
Aristophanes *Knights* 248	17
Catullus, poem 62	119
Demosthenes *On the Crown*	31
Homer, *Odyssey* 12.60–80	17
Homer, *Odyssey* 12.85	16
Ovid *Metamorphoses* 11.296	79

Ancient Document Index

Philo *Allegorical* 2.86   85
Philo *Allegorical* 3.189   44
Pindar *Olympian Ode* 1.18   41
Plutarch *Alexander* 52.1   31

Sophocles *Oedipus at Colonus*
lines 1630–40   117

Strabo *Geography*
16.2:28–30   61

Vergil *Georgics* 1.428–32   137

EARLY CHRISTIAN WRITINGS

Athanasius, *Festal Letter*   144

Eusebius *Historia Ecclesiae*
6.25.4   144

Hippolytus, *Apostolic Tradition*
6   56

Irenaeus *Against Heresies*
3.3–4   129

Origen *Homilies on Joshua*
18.2.3   20

www.ingramcontent.com/pod-product-compliance
Lightning Source LLC
Chambersburg PA
CBHW050810160426
43192CB00010B/1713